USDA

United States
Department of
Agriculture

Forest Service

Pacific Northwest
Research Station

General Technical Report
PNW-GTR-781

January 2009

Sampling and Estimation Procedures for the Vegetation Diversity and Structure Indicator

Bethany K. Schulz, William A. Bechtold, and Stanley J. Zarnoch

Authors

Bethany K. Schulz is a research ecologist, Pacific Northwest Research Station, Forestry Sciences Laboratory, 3301 C Street, Suite 200, Anchorage, AK 99503-3954; **William A. Bechtold** is a research forester, and **Stanley J. Zarnoch** is a mathematical statistician, Southern Research Station, 200 Weaver Blvd., Asheville, NC 28804.

Cover

Western hemlock forest near Hawk Mine, Alaska (photo by Jonathan Williams).

Abstract

Schulz, Bethany K.; Bechtold, William A.; Zarnoch, Stanley J. 2009.
Sampling and estimation procedures for the vegetation diversity and structure indicator. Gen. Tech. Rep. PNW-GTR-781. Portland, OR: U.S. Department of Agriculture, Forest Service, Pacific Northwest Research Station. 53 p.

The Vegetation Diversity and Structure Indicator (VEG) is an extensive inventory of vascular plants in the forests of the United States. The VEG indicator provides baseline data to assess trends in forest vascular plant species richness and composition, and the relative abundance and spatial distribution of those species, including invasive and introduced species. The VEG indicator is one of several sets of measures collected by the Forest Inventory and Analysis (FIA) Program of the USDA Forest Service to assess forest health. This document describes the sampling design, field data collection methods, primary output objectives, and estimation procedures for summarizing FIA VEG data.

Keywords: FIA, forest health monitoring, forest structure, forest vegetation, plot-based sampling, species composition, species distribution, species richness.

This paper was subjected to an anonymous peer-review process coordinated by an independent editor, and the manuscript has been modified accordingly.

Contents

Introduction

Forest Inventory and Analysis and Forest Health Indicators

The USDA Forest Service Forest Inventory and Analysis (FIA) Program has traditionally conducted timber inventories of the Nation's forests. Although the focus has historically been commodity driven, many researchers have recognized the utility of using FIA data to analyze wildlife habitat, range, recreation, hydrology, and more (Rudis 1991, 2003). Recently, a new enhanced FIA Program has been implemented to formally respond to customers' interest in nontimber attributes of forests (Bechtold and Patterson 2005). Integration with the Forest Health Monitoring (FHM) Program is the new component of FIA, providing a three-phase nationwide systematic sample of a wide array of forest ecosystem parameters.

The FHM Program, originally established in 1990 as a cooperative effort between the U.S. Environmental Protection Agency and the U.S. Forest Service, set about to establish measurable indicators of forest conditions (Riitters and Tkacz 2004). Forest health indicators include a broad suite of attributes that describe forests in terms of ownership, tree crown conditions, lichen community composition, down woody material, soil physical and chemical attributes, and vegetation diversity and structure. By measuring forest attributes consistently across the Nation, baseline estimates of each indicator can be established. The status and trends of those estimates can be monitored over time as they relate to changes in ecological conditions of the Nation's forests (Smith and Conkling 2004, Stapanian et al. 1997).

Vegetation is the source of primary production—the conversion of sunlight energy into energy stored as organic matter.

Vegetation as an Indicator of Forest Health

Vegetation is the source of primary production—the conversion of sunlight energy into energy stored as organic matter—and a fundamental determinant of habitat and wildfire fuel profile characterization. All plant communities are in flux; vegetation structural stages are often assessed to determine current potential for productivity and wildlife habitat. Disturbance of vegetation can have cascading effects through an ecosystem whether the changes are brought about gradually through natural succession or by sudden destructive events. Changes in species diversity and composition, structural diversity (Willis and Whittaker 2002), and the abundance of nonnative species are common national concerns, as reflected in the international criteria for assessing sustainability of forestry practices (USDA FS 1995).

The Vegetation Diversity and Structure (VEG) indicator embodies a set of measurements based on an inventory of vascular plants on an extensive systematic network of forest plots across the United States. The VEG indicator provides data to assess trends in forest vascular plant species richness and composition, the relative

Vegetation species composition data allow for species-based and community-based estimates at both the stand and population levels.

abundance and spatial distribution of those species, and overall physical structure created by the plant species present (Stolte et al. 2002). Data are also collected to describe vegetation community vertical structure and ground cover (i.e., soil/air interface).

Vegetation species composition data allow for species-based and community-based estimates at both the stand and population levels. Species-based estimates include individual species abundance (measured as the canopy cover of a species) and frequency (the distribution of a species across a specified area). Community-based estimates include the combination of species occurring within or across an area (i.e., species richness, composition, and stand structure). In addition, the site factor variables, other forest health indicator data, and other plot measurements can be used to assess species composition in relation to various environmental factors with multivariate analyses. Possible analyses include the examination of the distribution patterns of any species of interest (e.g., noxious, invasive, or introduced species), functional group (e.g., nitrogen fixers, wildfire accelerants or inhibitors), life form, or understory structure as it pertains to wildlife habitat, productivity, fuel profiles, or disturbance histories. With repeated measures on the same plots, VEG indicator data allow estimates of change from paired observations.

Long-term, large-scale vegetation inventory and monitoring programs are rare (Stohlgren 1994) but valuable for regional and national condition assessments. Such large-scale assessments provide broad overviews to help strategic policy development (Heinz Center 2006, Ingerson and Loya 2008) and allow land managers to place local assessments into regional or national perspectives, which facilitates the prioritization of limited resources available to managers. Reporting at local levels should be within the context of a larger region to clarify the status of a particular indicator within the smaller area because local levels may only be represented by a few plots that differ from the larger region. When trends or changes that warrant further investigation are detected, evaluation monitoring projects are initiated, often with intensified sampling effort at local levels, as the next step in forest health monitoring (Riitters and Tkacz 2004).

This document describes the sample design, primary output objectives, and estimation procedures for summarizing the VEG data. At the onset of this project, the intended audience was primarily FIA statisticians, analysts, and programmers. However, as more data become available, researchers and managers from other branches of the Forest Service, other agencies, nongovernment organizations, and universities should find this documentation useful.

The technical material in this document is divided into three main sections. The "Sample Design" section includes an overview of the FIA Program, a summary of the current field data collection methods, and specific issues related to collecting vegetation data on FIA plots. The "Plant Community Data Analysis" section provides background information on plant community analysis for analysts who are new to the subject, and the "Estimation" section defines plot- and population-level estimators and variances in equation form for statisticians and programmers.

Sample Design

Forest Inventory and Analysis Phases Defined

The three phases of the enhanced FIA Program are described in detail by Bechtold and Patterson (2005). The primary objective of phase 1 (P1) is to stratify land area in the population of interest for the purpose of reducing the variances of estimates. Phase 1 entails the use of ancillary data, including remotely sensed imagery in the form of aerial photography or satellite imagery, to stratify the land area in the population of interest and to assign plots to strata (two at minimum: forest and nonforest). Phase 2 (P2) entails visits by field crews to the physical locations of permanent ground plots to measure the traditional set of FIA variables such as forest type, site attributes, tree species, and tree size. The P2 sample is based on a nationwide hexagonal grid array of approximately 6,000-acre hexagons containing one permanent ground plot each. The primary objective of phase 3 (P3) is to measure additional variables related to the health of forest ecosystems. The P3 sample is a 1/16 subset of the P2 plot network, resulting in a sampling intensity of one plot per approximately 96,000 acres (38 400 hectares). Because P3 plots are also P2 plots, P3 measurements include all measurements made on P2 plots, plus measurement of the biotic and abiotic features associated with forest and ecosystem health. The VEG indicator set of measurements is collected on P3 plots.

Each permanent FIA ground plot consists of four 24-ft-radius (7.3-m) circular subplots arranged in a clustered formation (fig. 1). Additional areas within the subplots are used for various measurements. For the VEG indicator, three 3.28- by 3.28-ft (1 m^2) quadrats are established per subplot at 15 ft (4.56 m) from subplot center along transects at 30°, 150°, and 270°.

P3 Vegetation Indicator Method Basics

Sampling rules—

Permanent plots are established when at least one subplot in the plot configuration contains at least some accessible forest. Forested plots (or portions of plots) are considered inaccessible and not sampled if they are outside the U.S. boundary, access is denied by landowner, hazardous situations exist, or the area falls in census water (Bechtold and Patterson 2005).

The primary objective of phase 3 is to measure additional variables related to the health of forest ecosystems.

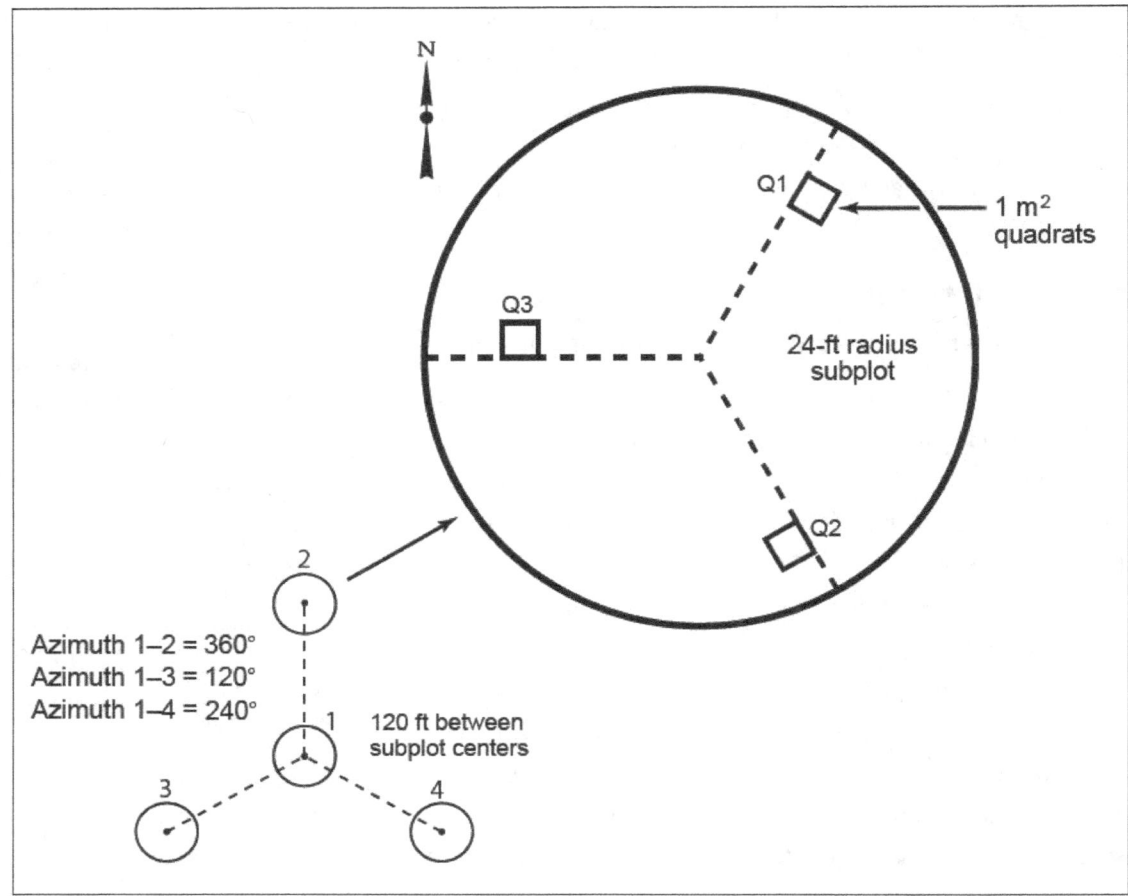

Figure 1—Arrangement of the Forest Inventory and Analysis plot design of four clustered subplots.

Vegetation is sampled only on land classified as accessible forest. Besides recording subplot area by land use, no measurements are taken on nonforested or inaccessible portions of a plot. No trees or other vegetation are measured in non-forest for two key reasons: (1) the FIA Program focuses on monitoring forest land and (2) data collection time is limited. Although extending P3 data to nonforest conditions has been considered, without P2 data collection, the augmenting environmental and mensuration variables would not be available. Although data from adjacent nonforested areas would be of interest to many users, sending the vegetation specialists into nonforested plant communities would increase their workload and time required on plot. In the future, some inventory units may opt to collect P2 data on nonforested lands, at which time it may be more practical to include P3 VEG data collection on nonforested lands.

Each plot is described by one or more "condition classes," which are delineated by variables that include land use, forest type, stand size, regeneration status, tree density, stand origin, ownership group, and disturbance history. When more than one distinct condition class is present on a plot, boundaries between them are mapped by the field crew collecting mensuration data (P2) for the plot. Mensuration data are stored by plot, subplot, and condition class to allow flexibility in summarizing population estimates by condition-class variables.

Although boundaries between forest and nonforest conditions are recognized by VEG field crews, boundaries between accessible forest conditions are ignored, and only one list of species is maintained for each quadrat and subplot. Assessing vegetation for each unique condition class would again require extra time and added complication. Still, subplots with multiple conditions often require special handling, as described in the "Estimation" section, and condition-class data from the P2 sample are required for compiling population estimates from the P3 VEG data. This is necessary to identify partially forested plots, and to permit analysis of subsets of forest (i.e., domains of interest), such as a particular forest type.

Sampling rules result in a mixture of plot configurations in the database:
1. Four complete subplots within 100-percent accessible forested conditions:
   a. In a single condition class
   b. More than one condition class
      i. Each subplot a single condition
      ii. One or more subplots with multiple conditions
2. Fewer than four subplots in accessible forested condition:
   a. In a single condition class
   b. More than one condition
      i. Each subplot a single condition
      ii. One or more subplots with multiple conditions
      iii. One or more subplots with less than 100-percent accessible forest land

Other permutations also exist; but the list above captures the general categories. This mixture of plot types presents a number of challenges for summarizing data at both plot and population levels. Ideally, every plot would be represented by four subplots in a single accessible forested condition. However, statistically based inventories capture conditions as they occur across the landscape.

Species data—
Each vascular plant species (including trees) with live stems within or foliage hanging over the forested portion of subplots is recorded. Plants identified to species are recorded with the accepted Natural Resources Conservation Service PLANTS database code (USDA NRCS January 2000 version). Plants not readily identified to species are assigned a genus or standard unknown code and are collected for identification if not locally sparse (five or fewer individual plants are present on the entire plot or immediate surrounding area).

For each species, the following data are recorded:

- Presence/absence on each quadrat
- Total aerial percentage canopy cover by species in 1-percent increments, based on the standard subplot area
- Percentage species canopy cover recorded by height layers, in the same increments and tolerances as described above
    - o Combined layers one and two (zero to 6 ft [0 to 1.83 m] from ground)
    - o Layer three (>6 to 16 ft [>1.83 to 4.88 m] from ground)
    - o Layer four (>16 ft [>4.88 m] from ground)

Crews begin by assessing species on quadrats for several reasons. Assessing the smaller quadrat areas as soon as possible before the vegetation is damaged or inadvertently trampled by other field crew members avoids sampling errors. Also, by focusing their eyes on smaller areas first, the vegetation specialists will notice small plant species or those that may become inconspicuous when assessing the much larger subplot area. Canopy cover is not recorded on quadrats, but each species recorded on a quadrat requires a cover measurement on the subplot. Quadrat species presence/absence data are used to describe the distribution of a species on a subplot, complementing the record of cover to describe its abundance.

On partially forested subplots where only the forested portions are assessed, all cover measurements are estimated based on the full subplot area. That is, if the cover of a species on the forested portion of the subplot is about equal to a circle with a radius of about 5.3 ft, cover is recorded as 5 percent ($\left(\frac{\pi(5.3)^2}{\pi(24)^2}\right) \times 100$) as it would be on a totally forested subplot.

Species abundance on partially forested subplots is collected this way primarily to accommodate measurement repeatability. Crews are trained to calibrate ocular estimates based on total subplot area, e.g., what 5-percent cover looks like on a regular, fully forested subplot. Subplots that are less than fully forested have variable proportions of forest. Estimating canopy cover over a consistent shape and area is less mentally taxing than having to adjust to smaller areas of variable shapes especially given that numerous estimates are made per subplot, and many plots are visited over the course of a season. Cover measurements on plots that are less than 100-percent forested are adjusted to relate only to the forested portion when estimates are computed.

To help standardize the sampling effort in the many different forest types across the country, a time limit is imposed for subplot species searches (time spent searching for additional species). This discourages the over-zealous crew member from searching for every last sprout and fosters the ability to fully sample as many subplots (and quadrats) as possible on very diverse or densely vegetated plots.

Vegetation structure and condition of soil/atmosphere interface—

On each subplot, several general assessments are made:

- **Percentage of subplot area in accessible forest land** is estimated because it affects data edit checks related to all ocular estimates. For example, the first two measures listed below are based on the percentage of the subplot area that is accessible forest; if the accessible forest is only 75 percent, the absolute canopy cover recorded by field crews cannot exceed 75 percent, and the sum of all ground variables must equal 75 percent.

- **Absolute canopy cover**, the canopy cover created by all plants present on a subplot, in 1-percent increments in each of four height layers
  o Layer one (0 to 2 ft [0 to 0.61 m] from ground)
  o Layer two (>2 to 6 ft [> 0.61 to 1.83 m] from ground)
  o Layer three (>6 to 16 ft [> 1.83 to 4.88 m] from ground)
  o Layer four (above 16 ft [> 4.88 m] from ground)
  This cannot be derived from species canopy cover because species cover may or may not overlap.

- **Ground variables** describe the soil/atmosphere interface in percentage cover of cryptobiotic crust, lichen, litter/duff, mineral soil, moss, road/trail, rock, standing water, permanent water, trash, and wood in 1-percent increments.

- **Nonforest land use** is recorded for any portion of the subplot not in the forested condition. Broad categories include agricultural uses, rangeland, development, and natural nonforest lands.

- **Condition class** information, such as forest type and stand size class is essential for compiling population estimates from VEG data and is collected by foresters as part of the P2 inventory.

On each quadrat, assessments include:

- The condition class the quadrat belongs to
- Level of trampling damage

Emphasis is made on completing the entire set of variables for a subplot when time limits restrict a crew from completing the entire plot, although this is rare. Subplots with complete measurements are more valuable for estimations and analysis than some data from all 12 quadrats with only one or two subplots complete, for example.

The complete P3 VEG field guide is posted on the FIA homepage http://www.fia.fs.fed.us/library/field-guides-methods-proc/ (USDA FS 2005).

Emphasis is made on completing the entire set of variables for a subplot when time limits restrict a crew from completing the entire plot.

Vegetation Inventory and Monitoring Issues

There are many ways to sample vegetation. When planning for vegetation sampling, investigators must consider the questions to address, the precision and accuracy required to answer those questions, and the ability to collect the needed data in the time allotted (Stohlgren 1994). Potential sources of error and measures to control or minimize this error should be documented. This section presents factors of the sampling design that have influenced the methods used for field data collection, given the logistical constraints of FIA inventories. It also addresses known sources of error and how they are addressed, including levels of species identification. Other investigators are welcome to use the P3 vegetation methods, but they are reminded that no one sampling method will meet all needs and are cautioned to carefully consider their own objectives before adopting the methods outlined in this document.

Sample design issues—

Geographic extent and spatial scale—The P3 grid is extensive; there is one plot per 96,000 acres. The FIA plot design is a cluster of four subplots; FIA's default estimation method for processing standard inventory (P2) data (Bechtold and Patterson 2005) combines subplot data to the plot level, ignoring the variance among subplots. Phase 3 VEG data do not necessarily need to be processed in this manner. Two considerations must be highlighted:

1. Plant species composition can be highly variable across much shorter distances than captured by the P3 sample. One objective of plant community analysis is to describe and explain the variable nature of species composition. Species composition in plots that straddle multiple forest types may be highly variable from subplot to subplot, but the between-subplot variability may be either greater or less than the variability among subplots of the same forest types on different plots. For example, consider two plots that both have some subplots in a Douglas-fir forest type and some subplots in aspen forest type. Even if the plots are a great distance from each other, the subplots in the Douglas-fir type often have species compositions that are more similar to Douglas-fir type in another plot than to the subplots in the aspen forest type on the same plot.

2. The VEG data are recorded only on the portions of a plot that are accessible and defined as forest. Where fewer than four subplots are forested, the measured subplots can still be combined for most plot and population estimates. Plots and subplots that are less than 100-percent forested should not be included in some VEG estimators because they need to be derived from sampling units of standard size. This is because the relationship between number of species and area sampled is not linear (Crawley and Harral

2001). Analysts may choose to include data from plots less than 100-pecent forested but should compare variances and note the types of plot configurations included in reported estimates. Details about the appropriateness of including partially forested samples are provided in the "Estimation" section.

Number and size of plots—Most vegetation inventory and monitoring projects determine the number and size of plots based on specific objectives of the project, and pilot studies are often used to optimize the plot configuration and sample size (Kenkel and Podani 1991). According to McCune and Grace (2002), the "many and small" scheme will yield accurate estimates of abundance for the most common species, but incomplete species lists. The "few and large" scheme results in a more complete species list but overestimates the abundance of rarer species. The FIA sample design—plots composed of a cluster of subplots—is a tradeoff between the two approaches.

For any subset of data subjected to analysis and summary, the population should be described in terms of numbers of full and partial plots and homogeneity of conditions found on those plots. Mixed-condition and partially forested plots should receive special consideration in plot summaries and population estimates, as described in the "Estimation" section.

Duration and remeasurement of site visits—Plots are usually visited on a single day every 5 to 10 years. Limited time on the plot and the phenological state of the vegetation will affect the thoroughness of the species list and the measures of species total cover. Limiting search times helps standardize the "sampling effort" for species lists. We acknowledge that percentage canopy cover for many species can change dramatically over very short periods during the growing season.

Ocular estimation issues—

Ocular canopy cover measures of abundance are commonly used in plant community analysis (Daubenmire 1959, Elzinga et al. 1998, McCune and Grace 2002, Mueller-Dombois and Ellenberg 1974). Although cover is a percentage of a standard area and therefore "absolute," it is not a precise measurement. Many studies have been conducted to evaluate the repeatability of canopy cover measures (Hatton et al. 1986, Helm and Mead 2004, Kennedy and Addison 1987, Sykes et al. 1983, van Hees and Mead 2000). These studies show that cover estimates are most variable at the moderate level (30 to 70 percent). Even though some may question the repeatability of canopy cover as an abundance measure, it has been shown to be reliable for species abundance in broad-scale studies encompassing a variety of plant communities (Mueller-Dombois and Ellenberg 1974). Most plant ecology studies

> **Limited time on the plot and the phenological state of the vegetation will affect the thoroughness of the species list and the measures of species total cover.**

9

employ cover classes when evaluating canopy cover with ocular estimates. Many cover class schemes that have been developed have smaller increments at either end of the scale and wide margins in the middle (McCune and Grace 2002). It is accepted that such schemes reduce variability issues among observers (Mueller-Dombois and Ellenberg 1974). Although species abundance in P3 VEG are recorded as percentage canopy cover "to the nearest 1 percent," measurement quality objectives tolerances for precision of field-collected data mimic cover classes described above. Analysts are cautioned that the raw data should be transformed to cover classes when applying multivariate methods. Use of raw data, or even midranges of cover classes, tend to overemphasize dominant species over those in the mid to low abundance classes (McCune and Grace 2002). Note that usually more than half of all species canopy cover measures in the VEG database are 1 percent.

Some researchers have suggested stem counts instead of canopy cover estimates. Although counts of individuals belonging to a single species are well-suited to specific monitoring efforts concerning rare species or treatment effects, they are very time-consuming and are generally limited to studies concerning a single or a few species on any given site (Elzinga et al. 1998). Counting individual plants is impractical and unnecessary for the objectives of the P3 VEG indicator. To further address this point, advantages and disadvantages of each method are tabulated below. When assessing species' distribution over space and time, a combination of cover and frequency gives a broader evaluation (Daubenmire 1959). The P3 VEG indicator measures generate both cover and frequency data.

The following tabulation shows the advantages and disadvantages of counts as a measure of vascular plant species abundance:

Advantages	Disadvantages
1. When used within a given area, quantifying the number of individual plants of a given species can give a complete census, and therefore, is not an estimate.	1. Difficult to use with clonal species (hard to distinguish individuals, e.g., rhizomatous grasses, aspen clones).
2. Preferred method for monitoring a single species, or a small group of species (i.e.,. trees on plot).	2. Accuracy can be poor owing to missed individuals (small individuals, individuals at different life stages).
3. Can be reported as numbers of individuals per unit area, so sample areas do not need to be equal to compare results from multiple sources.	3. Insensitive as a vigor-related measure in long-lived species, such as trees or shrubs.
	4. **Very** time consuming, especially when each species must be assessed over a fairly large area (subplot) and vegetation is dense. (This alone makes the method prohibitive on P3 plots, visited 1 day (4 to 6 hours) every 5, 7, or 10 years).

The following tabulation lists the advantages and disadvantages of canopy cover as a measure of vascular plant species abundance:

Advantages	Disadvantages
1. Expresses a species' "influence" on the area of interest.	1. Can change dramatically over the course of a growing season for most species other than dwarf shrubs and other low woody plants.
2. Does not require individual plants to be identified.	
3. Quantitative method that can be applied to just about all life forms; therefore, they can be evaluated with the same parameter. (Equalizes the contribution of small but abundant species with those that are larger but few.)	2. Visual estimates can differ among observers.
	3. Difficult to assess plants above 1 m in height (or waist height of observer).
4. Rapid visual evaluation of many species is possible.	
5. Widely used in ecological studies.	
6. Meets criteria for structural classification (spacing and height).	

(Summarized from Daubenmire 1959, Elzinga et al. 1998, Jukola-Sulonen and Salemaa 1985, McCune and Grace 2002, and Mueller-Dombois and Ellenberg 1974.)

Species identification issues—

Data are collected on all vascular plants rooted in or overhanging the forested subplot space. In addition to species that are overlooked because of low abundance or absence at the time of the plot visit (ephemerals), there may be species that cannot be identified because of phenological stage of development, sparse numbers of individuals for collection, or damaged condition. These factors are inherent in all plant surveys, and contribute to the uncertainty of species composition and richness estimates. There are accepted methods that account for undiscovered species in population estimation of gamma, as explained in the "Estimation" section. However, although it is rare for plant inventory and monitoring studies to report unidentified species as a source of error (Scott and Hallam 2002), FIA acknowledges and reports the percentage of species distinguished but not identified.

Steps are taken to maximize the quality of the data collected. Data are collected by specialists with prior botanical experience who are certified in the P3 VEG sampling methods. Repeatability studies on vegetation data collected by FIA have shown that crews on average identify 75 percent of plants to species, and 89 percent to genus. They agree on 71 percent of the species identifications, with most differences attributed to closely related species and plants overlooked because of low abundance (Gray and Azuma 2005). These results are similar to other vegetation inventory repeatability studies, but the expected repeatability in identification does affect the ability to track all species over time with the same reliability. Species that are frequently encountered or are abundant are likely to be identified correctly more often than those species that are very infrequent or present in trace amounts.

Crews collect specimens of plants they cannot readily identify unless the plant is locally sparse or in very poor condition for identification. If a plant species cannot be determined, genus or standard unknown codes are accepted. Standard unknown codes provide information about the plants' life form, which enables those records to be included in analysis of plant communities by life form and to contribute to species counts for any plot.

The incorporation of standard unknown codes (USDA NRCS 2000) has reduced the number of unknown codes that cannot be interpreted by anyone other than the person collecting data, and the total number of species per plot is tracked with the inclusion of a "unique species number" variable. A species list is maintained for each plot. When an unknown plant is first encountered, an unknown code is assigned (e.g., 2FDA, representing an annual dicot forb [all standard unknown codes begin with "2"]). A unique species number of "1" is assigned to the record. The next time the code 2FDA is entered on that plot, the field crew must consider "is this the same 2FDA as recorded earlier?" If yes, the same unique species number is assigned (1). If no (it is another unique species), a unique species number of "2" is assigned. The two species are distinguished by the unique species number maintained in the database, and the number of species observed on each plot is accurately recorded in the database, even if they are not all identified. This maintains the ability to count the number of distinguishable species per quadrat, subplot, and plot.

Use of general codes may cause underestimation of gamma diversity (number of unique species) because all the collective 2FDAs that remain in the database after all possible identifications are made do not represent the same species on different plots nor are they all unique species. However, they reduce the number of unknown codes that do not supply any information about the plant in question and that would inflate values of gamma. Prior to implementation of this scheme, gamma from data collected between 2001 and 2003 included 2,018 "free-form" distinct unknown codes. Many of these could have referred to the same species. That number was reduced to 27 when codes were converted to standardized unknown codes, resulting in reduction of population gamma while maintaining observed plot-level species richness (alpha)

Plant Community Data Analysis

The fundamental analysis goal of the VEG indicator is to assess vascular plant species assemblages in the Nation's forests. Data are compiled to describe the species encountered and the plant communities of the sampled area. Assessment objectives include estimation of plot-level and population-level attributes that serve as indicators of forest condition (e.g., individual species distribution and abundance, species diversity, stand physical structure) and pattern recognition (e.g., presence and abundance of introduced species, community type descriptions, and indicator species analysis).

The FIA plot design (fig. 1) spreads four subplots over an area larger than would be sampled by a single plot of equivalent size. As a result, plots are "homogenized" and the between-plot variance of P2 timber volume estimates is reduced, thus reducing the number of plots needed to achieve a given accuracy standard (Bechtold and Patterson 2005). Somewhat in contrast, the aim of plant community analyses is to capture and explain the variability observed, and thereby increase the ability to predict where similar patterns in species composition may occur. The four-subplot plot design can blur the lines between distinct plant communities that may occur on a plot and decrease the resolution of the sample for plant community analysis. These differences, the different intensities of the sampling grids, and logistic constraints, all influence the type of estimations possible from each phase of the forest inventory.

The sparse nature of the P3 sample makes it most appropriate for national or regional population reporting. When data are stratified by forest type after collection and reported at the scale of an ecological region, variances may be reduced. Ecological provinces, as described by Bailey (1995) and Cleland et al. (2005), define areas with similar physical and biological features that influence vegetation and are also appropriate for defining populations for which reliable estimates can be made. However, because permanent plots are installed and revisited over time, stand-level changes can be assessed and reported at a local level and compared to changes over a larger region.

Differences in the distribution and abundance of individual species, and differences in composition and structure between and within plots can be examined. Indicator species analysis can be applied to determine if a species of interest has an affinity for unique environmental conditions (Klinka et al. 1989, McCune and Grace 2002). Trend and pattern analyses across time and space are possible by calculating similarity between plots based on species composition and site environmental data.

This section describes the nature of plant community data, concepts of the individual attributes assessed, and the utility of species composition data. Detailed equations for the estimators and their variances are provided in the next section. The various basic estimators for the VEG indicator are listed in table 1.

Table 1—Summary of vegetation indicator estimators and appropriate sampling units

	Plot level	Population level
Describing individual species observed		
Species distribution	Frequency	Frequency
	Quadrat	Quadrat
	Subplot	Subplot
		Plot
Species abundance	Average % cover	Average % cover
	Average % cover by layer	Average % cover by layer
Describing plant communities		
Diversity		
Species richness[a]	Average quadrat alpha	Average quadrat alpha
	Average subplot alpha	Average subplot alpha
	Plot alpha	Average plot alpha
Total number of species	Plot gamma	Gamma
		Jackknife estimates
Differential	Plot beta	Population beta
Structure		
Absolute cover[b]	Average % cover 0-2 ft	Average % cover 0-2 ft
	Average % cover 2-6 ft	Average % cover 2-6 ft
	Average % cover 6-16 ft	Average % cover 6-16 ft
	Average % cover 16+ ft	Average % cover 16+ ft
Ground cover[c]	Average % cover	Average % cover

[a] Number of species per standard area.
[b] All species over subplot area.
[c] Various descriptors over subplot area.

The Nature of Plant Community Data

A species inventory indicates how many species are contained within an ecological unit or population of interest, and the species lists for individual plots allow analysts to assess how those species are grouped or distributed over the area of interest. A species matrix—a table of species recorded by sample unit (plot, subplot, or quadrat)—is the basic data building block used to describe both the individual plots and species' distributions over a population area of interest (table 2). However, multiple species create highly multivariate data. Whereas some groups of plots will have species composition that is very similar, other such groups will have no species in

Some variation in species composition is due to environmental factors; other sources of variation include chance, local disturbances, and the statistical limitations of sampling.

Table 2—Sample species matrix with presence-absence data

Species	Plot 1	Plot 2	Plot 3	Plot 4	...	Plot n
Sp1	0	1	1	0	...	1
Sp2	1	1	0	1	...	1
Sp3	1	0	1	0	...	1
...	...	...	...	...	...	...
Sps	0	1	0	1	...	0

common. Some variation in species composition is due to environmental factors; other sources of variation include chance, local disturbances, and the statistical limitations of sampling. As the species matrix grows to include more plots over larger areas and more variable conditions, it becomes increasingly "sparse," with many zeros, because most species occur on only a small portion of plots. This leads to high coefficients of variation and lack of normality, limiting the applicability of normal-theory multivariate methods. Despite this, there are many ways to summarize and analyze data to provide useful information.

Attributes to Assess as Indicators

Individual species distribution—

The full inventory of vascular plants on forested plots provides, at a most basic level, information on where a species occurs and where it is absent. Presence/absence (P/A) information is used to describe how the observed species are dispersed over an area of interest. It is useful in large-scale projects where vegetation composition changes dramatically across the area of interest (McCune and Grace 2002). Although P/A data are very simplistic, they cannot be extracted from surveys that only record a limited subset of the actual species present (e.g., surveys that record only the most abundant species or species on a list). The P/A data can be expressed as relative frequency; the ratio of the number of sample or subsample units where a species was recorded to the number of total sample or subsample units visited (table 3). Relative frequency will be referred to as simply "frequency" throughout this document.

Frequency—Frequency describes the distribution patterns of a species on a plot or within a stand, i.e., clumped vs. dispersed (Elzinga et al. 1998). Frequency is often calculated from data collected at multiple scales and is most informative when reported at multiple scales (table 3). Frequency is used for change detection in species' spatial distribution over time; this is especially useful for monitoring invasive species (fig. 2). For the VEG indicator, frequency measures are more reliable than cover measures for detecting change. Species cover can vary greatly owing to phenological changes throughout a growing season (Smith et al. 1986) and climatic variations from year to year, whereas frequency reflects where a species is rooted on a set of permanent (revisited) plots.

Frequency is dependent on the size of the area sampled (McCune and Grace 2002) and, thus, frequency estimates should be based on fixed-area samples. For the VEG indicator, this is problematic because partially forested plots cause variations in the area from which vegetation is sampled. Estimations can be made by

Table 3—Distribution of selected native (N) and introduced (I) species over 915 plots

Number of plots	Growth habit	Scientific name[a]	Common name	Origin	Constancy[b] over all 915 plots	Plots where present		
						Average cover	Subplot frequency	Quadrat frequency
					Percent			
376	Vine	*Parthenocissus quinquefolia* L.	Virginia creeper	N	41.09	6.53	0.79	0.36
324	Tree	*Acer rubrum* L.	red maple	N	35.41	15.10	0.77	0.33
297	Shrub, vine	*Toxicodendron radicans* (L.) Kuntz	eastern poison ivy	N	32.46	7.90	0.63	0.21
274	Tree	*Quercus rubra* L.	northern red oak	N	29.95	10.40	0.59	0.09
215	Vine, shrub	*Rosa multiflora* Thunb. ex Murr.	multiflora rose	I	23.50	7.83	0.62	0.16
159	Tree, shrub	*Sassafras albidum* (Nutt.) Nees	sassafras	N	17.38	8.90	0.72	0.21
77	Graminoid	*Achnatherum hymenoides* (Roemer & J.A. Schultes) Barkworth	Indian ricegrass	N	8.42	1.51	0.64	0.11
77	Graminoid	*Bromus tectorum* L.	cheatgrass	I	8.42	4.46	0.72	0.33
75	Shrub	*Lonicera canadensis* Bartr. ex Marsh	American fly honeysuckle	N	8.20	2.63	0.60	0.11
52	Subshrub	*Mahonia repens* (Lindl.) G. Don	creeping barberry	N	5.68	2.79	0.62	0.25
51	Vine	*Lonicera japonica* Thunb.	Japanese honeysuckle	I	5.57	16.90	0.64	0.34
49	Forb/herb	*Daucus carota* L.	Queen Anne's lace	I	5.36	3.86	0.50	0.18
49	Forb/herb	*Phytolacca americana* L.	American pokeweed	N	5.36	3.57	0.46	0.07
41	Forb/herb	*Alliaria petiolata* (Bieb.) Cavara & Grande	garlic mustard	I	4.48	8.85	0.67	0.33
41	Forb/herb	*Apocynum androsaemifolium* L.	spreading dogbane	N	4.48	1.70	0.50	0.16
41	Forb/herb	*Circaea lutetiana* L.	enchanter's nightshade	N	4.48	2.36	0.62	0.22
41	Forb/herb	*Leucanthemum vulgare* Lam.	oxeye daisy	I	4.48	2.10	0.47	0.11
41	Forb/herb	*Sanguinaria canadensis* L.	bloodroot	N	4.48	2.20	0.49	0.10

[a] USDA NRCS 2000.
[b] Constancy is the percentage of plots where recorded (plot frequency x 100).

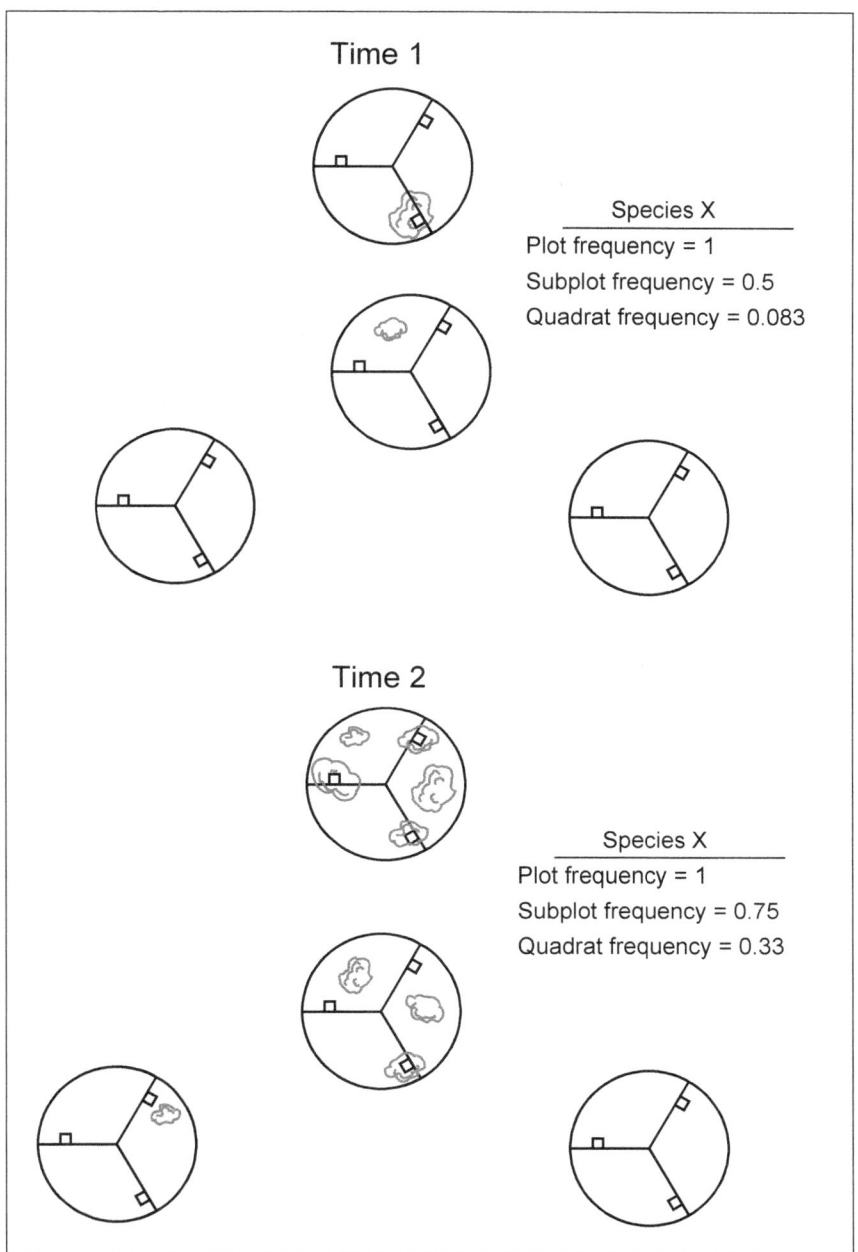

Figure 2—Frequency tracks change in species distribution over time. For purposes of the P3 VEG indicator, frequency is defined as the ratio of the number of plots, subplots, or quadrats where a species was recorded to the number of plots, subplots, or quadrats visited.

using only 100-percent accessible forested subplots or plots (to adhere to standard size area), or by using all plots visited, including those that are not fully forested. Additional information provided by data collected on sample units that are less than 100-percent accessible forest is captured when estimates are computed from all plots and subplots visited. To illustrate the difference between estimates using "full" and "all" plots, consider multiflora rose, (*Rosa multiflora* Thunb. ex Murr.), an important invasive species in the Eastern United States: results from data collected between 2001 and 2004 show this species has a plot frequency of 0.176, based on plots composed of four fully forested subplots, whereas its plot frequency based on all plots, regardless of percentage of accessible forest, is 0.249, indicating it is often found on forest edges. Analysts would miss this indication of a species invasion pattern if limited to observing frequencies based on 100-percent forested plots, especially when summarizing results over large geographic regions.

For purposes of the P3 VEG indicator, frequency is defined as the proportion of plots, subplots, or quadrats where a species was recorded (fig. 2 and table 3). Constancy is another way to express frequency, where the proportion is simply multiplied by 100 and expressed as the **percentage** of sample units where the species was recorded. Constancy is used along with cover measures when describing plant community composition (i.e., DeVelice et al. 1999, Johnson and Swanson 2005, Tart et al. 2005) and is also useful for reporting a species distribution on very broad scales. When reporting results, analysts must distinguish if all plots or only full plots are included.

Individual species abundance—
Species abundance is recorded as aerial canopy cover (two-dimensional view from directly above) for total cover. Vertical arrangement is obtained by estimating canopy cover by individual height layers. These abundance measures are used to assess species' relative abundance to each other, classify plots into community types (Tart et al. 2005), and describe plant community structure in terms of species distribution both horizontally and vertically. This information can be used to characterize wildlife habitat (Cooperrider et al. 1986, MacArthur and MacArthur 1961), wildland fuel profiles (Greenough 2001, Lutes et al. 2003), and impacts of disturbance, including invasive species. Ocular estimation of percentage canopy cover is the most common approach among ecologists to measuring species abundance (McCune and Grace 2002). Ocular estimates are quick and nondestructive, providing efficient assessments of abundance. Note, however, that although canopy cover measures are absolute in terms of percentage of a given area, they should not be considered to be precise.

Ocular estimates are quick and nondestructive, providing efficient assessments of abundance.

Species average cover—The average cover of an individual species is compiled from raw subplot data. Cover values are summed and then divided by the number of subplots in the sample, both for plot-level and population-level estimates.

Users must be cautioned that population estimates over large regions are likely to have high variances, given the extensive nature of the P3 grid. This is also a reflection of nonrandom spatial distribution of plant species. Species may occur in high abundance in a few places and in low abundance (or absent) in most others, so that there are many plots where a species was not recorded. Although it is possible to compile average cover on national or regional scales, it is generally more informative to define a population in more specific terms, such as in a particular forest type within a particular EcoProvince.

For some purposes, a more informative description of species abundance within a population of interest is compiled from only the plots where the species was observed (no zero values are included). This convention is sometimes used to summarize and describe floristic composition in plant-community type classifications, and is usually compiled after a community classification exercise. Constancy can be reported along with species average cover to reflect how often that species was recorded within the plots of a community type (defined in the classification exercise). Another example of this application is for reporting species distribution summaries over broad scales, as shown in table 3.

Species average cover by layer—To describe a species' vertical distribution, cover is reported for each of three general height layers (0 to 6 ft, 6 to 16 ft, and above 16 ft). The objective is to describe how that species is distributed throughout the height layers when the species is recorded (fig. 3). This provides information useful for fuels or wildlife habitat characterization.

Diversity of plant communities—

Species diversity can be assessed in a number of ways, based on the scope and scale of an inventory project or plant community study (Conkling et al. 2005, Ludwig and Reynolds 1988, McCune and Grace 2002, Pitkanen 1998, Whittaker 1975). Traditionally, diversity is composed of two distinct components: species richness (the total number of species) and evenness (how abundant each species is relative to other species). Diversity indices attempt to combine these two components, but are difficult to interpret because they combine, and therefore confound, a number of variables (Ludwig and Reynolds 1988). Diversity indices such as Simpson's index, Shannon-Wiener index, and Hill numbers may be of interest when the plot grid is intensified, as in special projects. These indices lose meaning at the extensive scale

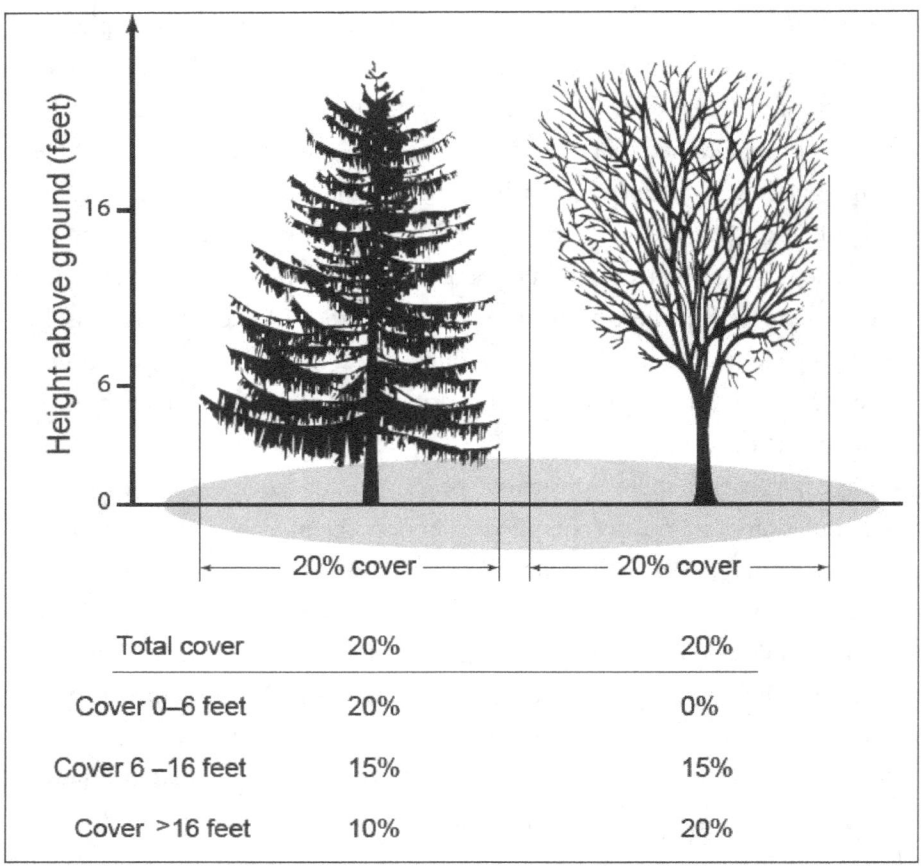

Total cover	20%	20%
Cover 0–6 feet	20%	0%
Cover 6 –16 feet	15%	15%
Cover >16 feet	10%	20%

Figure 3—Species cover by height layers provides information on each species contribution to stand structure. Although figure shows individual plants, a single cover estimate is recorded to include all plants of a given species.

> The total number of species in a population of interest is the most fundamental and easily interpretable measure of diversity.

of the P3 grid, and the concepts are difficult to explain (McCune and Grace 2002). However, the VEG indicator species composition data do provide data on both species richness and abundance, and users have the option to explore the use of diversity indices for specific applications, if desired.

Standard estimators of diversity for P3 VEG data concentrate instead on basic species richness and differential diversity, the differences in species composition between sampling units or populations. These can be expressed at a number of scales as will be described.

Species richness—The total number of species in a population of interest is the most fundamental and easily interpretable measure of diversity. It is most meaningful when the sample units are equivalent in terms of sample area as well as time spent searching. There are two common measures of species richness; alpha and gamma diversity.

Alpha diversity is traditionally defined as species richness, the number of species per unit area. For the VEG indicator, alpha can be reported at multiple scales: quadrat (10.76 ft^2 or 1 m^2), subplot area (24^2 πft^2), or plot area (4 x 24^2 πft^2). Because unit area must be held constant, only whole subplots and plots should be used for plot- or population-level estimates. Alphas based on each of these sizes are used to describe and compare species richness at multiple scales in different ecological regions or forest types (fig. 4).

Gamma diversity is the total number of unique species recorded in the population of interest.

Both alpha and gamma diversity can be summarized by proportion of native and introduced species, and plants not identified to species. Table 4 shows how gamma can be reported in terms of native, introduced, and species of unknown origin for various community types.

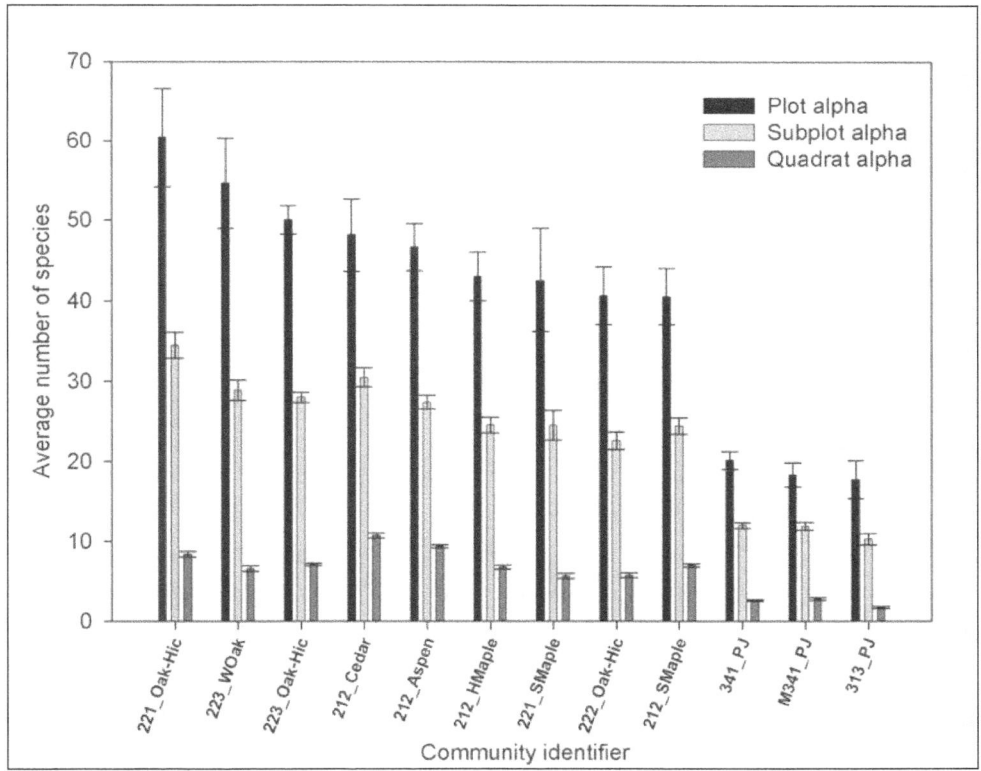

Figure 4—Average plot, subplot, and quadrat alphas for 12 populations defined by forest types within ecological provinces. Error bars show plus and minus one standard error. See table 4 for explanation of codes.

Table 4—Species richness and nativity of identified species for 12 ecological province/forest type pairs represented by fully forested plots

Ecological province (code)[a] and forest type	Plots (n)	Mean plot alpha ($\hat{A}''$)	Gamma[b] (γ)	Plants identified to species		Unknown origin[c]
				Native	Introduced	
Number of species						
Laurentian mixed forest (212):						
Northern white-cedar	13	50.0	270	221	10	39
Sugar maple/beech/birch	28	42.8	335	256	25	54
Hard maple/basswood	14	44.9	271	203	13	55
Aspen	33	48.8	438	325	39	74
Eastern broadleaf forest (221):						
White oak/red oak/hickory	10	62.6	250	178	23	49
Sugar maple/beech/birch	11	43.5	201	135	14	52
Midwest broadleaf forest (222):						
White oak/red oak/hickory	10	41.8	218	161	20	37
Central interior broadleaf forest (223):						
White oak/red oak/hickory	42	53.3	470	352	24	94
White oak	10	59.6	262	199	11	52
Colorado plateau semidesert (313):						
Pinyon/juniper woodland	12	17.9	98	76	5	17
Interior semidesert and desert (341):						
Pinyon/juniper woodland	34	20.5	248	194	9	45
Nevada-Utah mountain semidesert coniferous forest (M341):						
Pinyon/juniper woodland	13	18.5	100	78	1	21

[a] Ecoolgical province codes are used in figure 4 to simplify labels.
[b] Gamma represents the total number of unique plant codes recorded in a community, including codes for plants identified to species or genus, and symbols for plants that cannot be identified to genus.
[c] Unknown origin includes plants not identified to species.

Unobserved species are a factor in any inventory (Chao et al. 2000, Colwell et al. 2004, Heltshe and Forrester 1983). This is especially true when assessing all forest vascular plant species at the geographical extent and spatial scale of the FIA P3 sample; it is not expected that this inventory will encounter all possible species. There are methods to estimate the "true" number of species in a given population, such as extrapolating from species-area curves, parametric methods that are dependent on counts of individuals, and nonparametric estimators (McCune and Grace 2002, Scheiner 2003). Comparing species richness of two or more populations must address the differences in the sample sizes representing the populations; rarefaction methods allow for such comparisons (Gotelli and Colwell 2001, Koellner et al. 2004). This is discussed in more detail in the "Estimation" section.

Beta diversity—Beta diversity can be calculated a number of ways; in any of its forms, it describes differential diversity, the extent to which species composition and abundance differ from one place to another (Scheiner 2003, Whittaker et al.

2001). For the VEG indicator, it describes the degree of change in species composition between or within sample units or populations (Whittaker et al. 2001) and is calculated as the ratio of species richness of the total area sampled to the average number of species in the smaller individual samples. It is a measure of species heterogeneity across a population, and an index of the number of distinct communities present in the sample (Conkling et al. 2005, McCune and Grace 2002, Wilson and Shmida 1984).

Structure and condition of soil-atmosphere interface—
In addition to species data, the VEG indicator collects data on overall structure and conditions of the soil-atmosphere interface on each subplot. These data, along with variables collected on plots by P2 mensuration crews and other P3 indicators, describe environmental conditions on the plot and can be used as explanatory variables for multivariate analysis.

Absolute canopy cover by layer—These ocular estimates across the subplot area by four height layers (0 to 6 ft, 2 to 6 ft, 6 to 16 ft, and above 16 ft) assess the canopy cover of all vascular plants, regardless of species present or the amount of overlapping vegetation within a given layer. This cannot be derived directly from species canopy cover because species' cover may or may not overlap. Results are summarized either for the plot or population of interest. This basic assessment is useful for evaluating wildfire fuel characteristics and wildlife habitat.

Ground cover—Ground (soil-air interface) conditions are recorded as percentage cover of cryptobiotic crust, lichen, litter/duff, mineral soil, moss, road/trail, rock, standing water, permanent water, trash, and wood at the subplot level. These measurements are used to describe the physical conditions of the plot in terms of space available for vascular plant establishment. These data are used to populate an environmental matrix that describes physical features that potentially control or predict the plant species occurring on the plot (McCune and Grace 2002).

Plant Community Analysis

Species' distributions and abundance are fundamental to understanding patterns of communities and their relations to environmental conditions (Ludwig and Reynolds 1988, McCune and Grace 2002). One of the most basic steps in vegetation analyses is classification of community types. Classification is the process of grouping similar entities together into classes based on selected shared characteristics (Tart et al. 2005). In the case of plant communities, vegetation and environmental features are used to describe units that are useful for management applications (Boggs 2000).

Species' distributions and abundance are fundamental to understanding patterns of communities and their relations to environmental conditions.

Management applications that use classification information include describing the variety of vegetation communities occupying an area, characterizing the effect of disturbance or management on plant species, assessing resource conditions and risks, reporting presence and relative abundance of introduced species, developing wildfire-fuels-related analysis products, and enhancing effective communication between land managers (Tart et al. 2005).

Species composition data from FIA P2 plots only include tree species. These data are amenable to community classification, but typically can only be used to help define relatively broad types, e.g., at the group level of the revised U.S. National Vegetation Classification (USNVC) (FGDC 2007). Tree data can often be used to assign plots to alliances with existing USNVC keys (Faber-Langendoen and Menard 2006). However, additional data at the P3 level would provide a much stronger basis for developing types and assigning plots to existing types. In fact, the P3 plots could help validate P2-based decisions. The P3 VEG data can be used to further refine pre-assigned community types (e.g., forest types within a particular ecological province) and new classifications can be formulated by assessing similarities of sample unit species composition by using multivariate clustering techniques. Vegetation indicator data meet the requirements for the USNVC standards (FGDC 2007, Jennings et al. 2006). Clients and cooperators are interested in data generated by the VEG indicator for its use in classification.

The first step in classification, as with most multivariate analysis methods, is to compute similarities or "distances" between sample units. Similarity or distance measures are used to compare the species assemblages or site environmental data of two or more communities of interest. Classic methods for computing similarities include Jaccard (1901) and Sørenson (1948), among others. New approaches for assessing similarity of species compositions are being developed (Chao et al. 2005). Many are applicable to VEG indicator data. Clustering techniques can then be used to assign sample units into groups or classes.

Explanatory variables for species compositional differences must be considered at the scale of comparisons: regional or continental scales may be well explained by climatic variability, but landscape and local differentiation may be better explained by recent disturbances, local soil gradients, or other local geographic variants (Whittaker et al. 2001). The species and environmental data from the P3 VEG Indicator and other corresponding data for P3 plots generate complex data matrices that can be analyzed by multivariate techniques to discover and explore these trends.

Methods of analysis have rapidly evolved in recent years for relating species composition, abundance, and environmental data through the use of cluster analyses, ordination, and other multivariate methods (Frelich et al. 2003, McCune and Grace 2002, Nygaard and Ødegaard 1999, Pausas and Austin 2001, Pitkanen 1997, Scheller and Mladenoff 2002). Multivariate methods reduce complex data sets involving a large number of variables over many sample units into fewer synthesized or derived variables over groups of observations so that relationships may be revealed. Reducing complex data sets into fewer dimensions is useful for revealing patterns and trends (Ludwig and Reynolds 1988). Differences in the performance of individual species, and differences in composition and structure between sample units can be examined. Indicator species analysis can be applied to determine if a species of interest has an affinity for unique environmental conditions (Klinka et al. 1989, McCune and Grace 2002).

Change over time in multiple variables or estimators can also be explored by using multivariate methods that integrate the responses of the individual variables (McCune and Grace 2002). Species matrices at time t and time $t+1$ are tested for distances (dissimilarity) by using the Mantel test (McCune and Grace 2002, McCune and Mefford 1999). Differences in species composition can be compared with differences in environmental measures (ground cover, total foliar cover by layer, and applicable P2 attributes, for example) to examine the relations between changing plant communities and other measured variables (i.e., what controls overall species diversity, what physical features predict where changes will occur in the future?).

The process of multivariate analysis is usually iterative. For some analyses, data are transformed (e.g., converting cover measures to cover classes), relativized, or normalized; species lists are reduced; different approaches to determining similarities and clustering can be applied; and various ordination techniques can be tested. True patterns and trends will usually be revealed by using various techniques but may be best conveyed with one or two approaches. It is essential for analysts to keep track of the steps they use so they can be repeated as necessary and reported with results. Analysts should seek formal training in multivariate techniques if they are not familiar with them. There are numerous multivariate software packages available, but user-friendly software does not guarantee appropriate application of techniques.

Although multivariate methods can be useful for discovering patterns, they are difficult to apply to hypothesis testing in a direct manner. Emerging methodologies may provide univariate estimates for diversity patterns (Scheiner 1992), and analysts are encouraged to explore these methods as they become available.

Although multivariate methods can be useful for discovering patterns, they are difficult to apply to hypothesis testing in a direct manner.

Estimation

> **Plot-level estimators are generally most useful for mapped products; population-level estimators are generally most useful for tabular output.**

The estimators presented here are separated into two major types: (1) those that describe the distribution and abundance of individual plant species (i.e., species-based estimators) and (2) those that describe the plant community within the area sampled in terms of diversity and structure (i.e., community-based estimators). Estimators produced from VEG data yield output for mapped products (figs. 5 and 6), as well as standard tables for state, regional, and national reports (tables 3 and 4). Plot-level estimators are generally most useful for mapped products; population-level estimators are generally most useful for tabular output. This section proceeds with a discussion of species-based and community-based estimators, at the plot and population levels.

The VEG species data recorded for each plot are stored at the level at which they were collected: plots, subplots, and quadrats. General descriptions of the sampled area such as condition-class data are obtainable from ancillary P2 data sets so that data can be identified, selected, and compiled to create estimates for various populations and domains of interest. Ecoregion designations to subsection are available at the plot level, providing additional ancillary data at regional and landscape scales. Additional ancillary information from other P3 indicators and geographic information systems (GIS) can also be used, but exact plot locations are usually required for use of ancillary GIS data.

Ratios of Means

All of the estimators described here are based on ratio-of-means (ROM) estimators (Cochran 1977: section 6.2). These estimators are very similar to those used by FIA to process P2 inventory data (Bechtold and Patterson 2005), but simpler because they do not require stratified estimation, and they avoid a complicated adjustment (involving per-unit-area estimators and partial plots that straddle population boundaries), which is not necessary for any of the VEG estimators. This simplified approach is advantageous in that it does not require any data from FIA's phase 1 sample and can use software available in existing statistical packages such as SAS PROC SURVEYMEANS (SAS Institute Inc. 2004). The main disadvantage is that the double sampling for stratification technique used by FIA reduces the variance associated with many P2 estimators and would likely yield similar results for at least some of the VEG estimators. If P1 data are available and variance reduction through stratified sampling is of major concern to the analyst, the stratified estimation process described in Bechtold and Patterson (2005) may be applied to the VEG data. SAS PROC SURVEYMEANS also has the capability to incorporate stratification, which may be a simpler alternative to those who prefer to use stratified sampling.

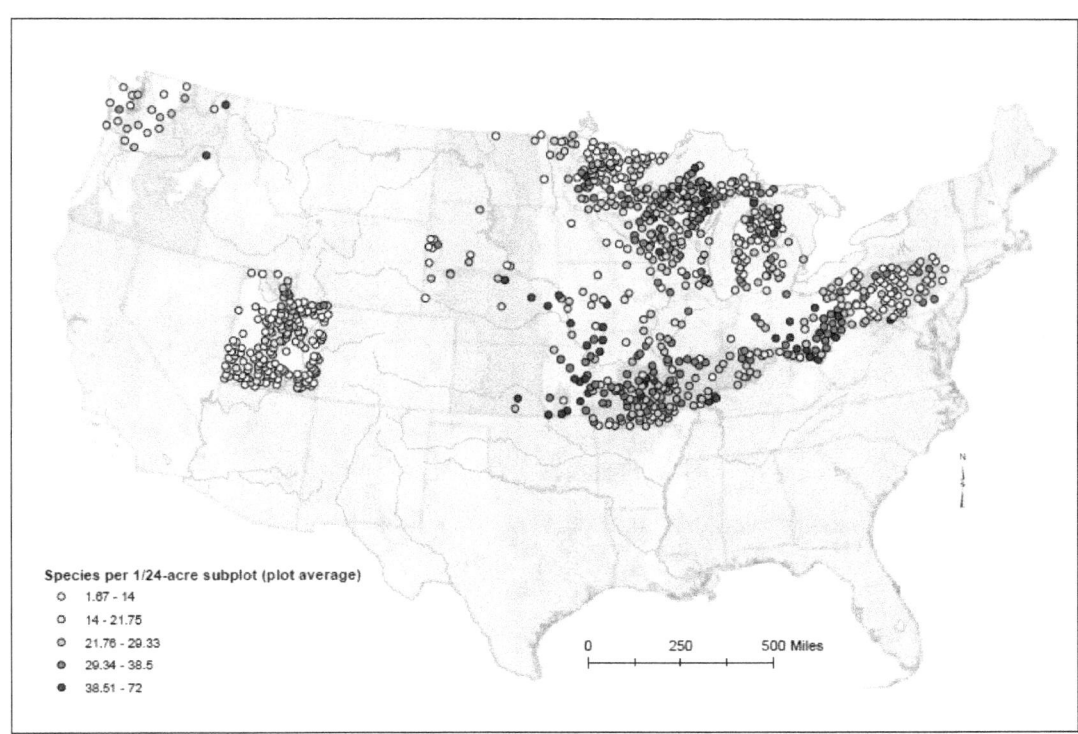

Figure 5—Plot average of subplot species richness. Plot locations are approximate.

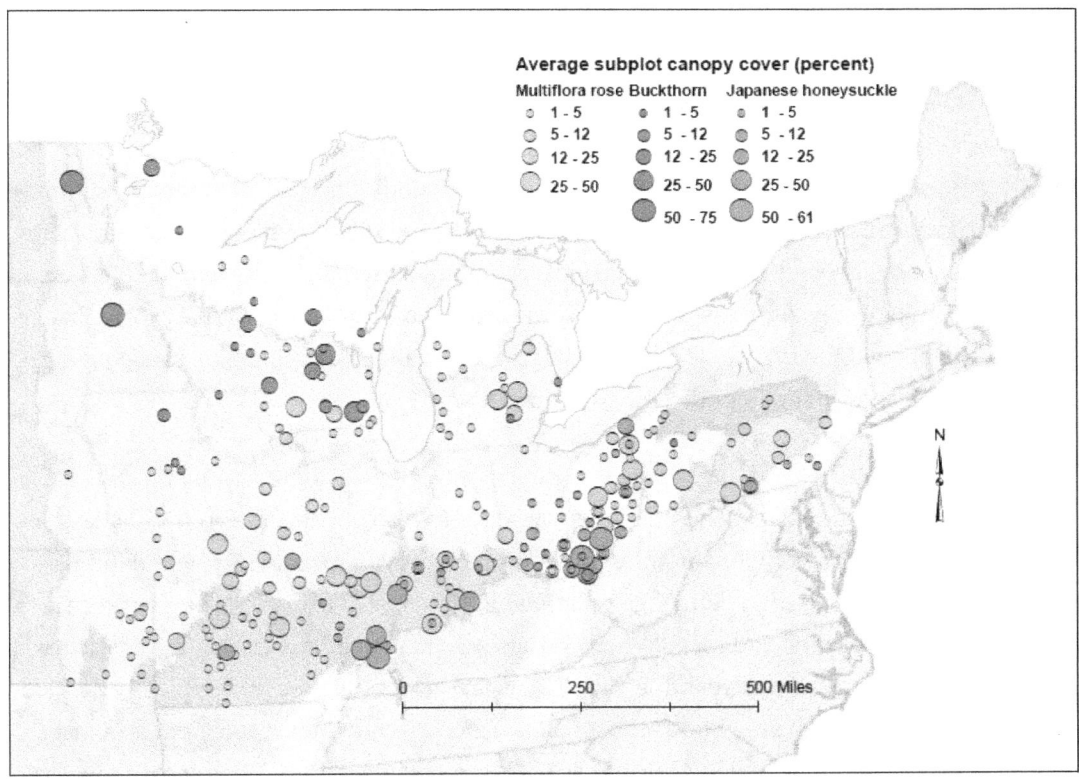

Figure 6—Distribution and average subplot cover of selected shrub species on plots where present. Northeastern United States. Plot locations are approximate.

The basic ROM estimator is specified as

$$\hat{R} = \frac{\overline{y}}{\overline{x}} = \frac{\sum\limits_{c=1}^{n} y_c}{\sum\limits_{c=1}^{n} x_c} \qquad (1)$$

with estimated variance

$$\hat{V}(\hat{R}) = \frac{1}{n(n-1)\,(\sum\limits_{c=1}^{n} x_c / n)^2} \left[\sum\limits_{c=1}^{n} y_c^2 + \hat{R}^2 \sum\limits_{c=1}^{n} x_c^2 - 2\hat{R}\sum\limits_{c=1}^{n} y_c x_c \right] \qquad (2)$$

where

y_c = the variable of interest observed on cluster c,

x_c = an auxiliary variable observed on cluster c that is correlated with y_c,

n = the number of clusters associated with the estimator of interest in the population of interest.

The estimators produced from equations (1) and (2) are either plot-level or population-level means. Plot-level means are averaged across the observations obtained from each of the four subplots, so the number of clusters (n) equals four. Population-level means are averaged from observations obtained from plots, so for population-level means the number of clusters (n) equals the number of plots in the population of interest. Note that n defined in this manner accounts for the first-stage clustering of observations resulting from the nested sampling design, where subplots are clustered on plots and quadrats are clustered on subplots. When n relates to subplots, observations are either observed directly from each subplot, or summarized across the quadrats on each subplot. When n relates to plots, observations are either observed directly from the plot, or summarized across the four subplots on that plot (or in some cases summarized across the 12 quadrats on that plot). Clustering beyond the first stage is ignored because the added complication rarely changes variance estimates significantly (Cochran 1977: 279).

Populations and Domains

The distinction between population variables (which are also referred to as design variables) and domain variables is also important with respect to n. Population variables are used to define the population of interest. They are known **before** the sampling occurs, and include such variables as state, county, ecological province, inventory panel, and year. For FIA P2 estimation, populations are typically defined as counties (Bechtold and Patterson 2005). For P3 estimates, ecological provinces (Bailey 1995, Cleland et al. 2005) are often more appropriate. Ecological provinces have similar physical and biological features that influence vegetation, and are often more meaningful than political boundaries when reporting results of VEG analyses.

Domain variables are not part of the sampling design, and their values are not known before sampling occurs. The condition-class variables collected by FIA (i.e., land use, forest type, stand size, regeneration status, tree density, stand origin, ownership group, and disturbance history) qualify as domain variables. Domains can also include other attributes that are measured (e.g., percentage slope) or computed from tree data (e.g., percentage stocking) or VEG data (e.g., plant community type as defined by classification exercises).

By definition, all domains of interest must be contained within the population of interest. However, some domains in the population of interest are not domains of interest. Note that all observations within the population of interest contribute to n, even those observations that are not in the domain of interest (e.g., nonforest). Also note that for plot-level estimators, the plot is defined as the population of interest.

Partial Plots and Subplots

Analyses can become complicated when plots or subplots are partially forested or otherwise fall into multiple condition classes (i.e., domains). Some of these estimators require that 100 percent of a subplot or 100 percent of a plot must be within the domain of interest because it is important to restrict observations to areas of uniform size. Partially forested observations are thus excluded from certain estimations because no VEG data are recorded in nonforest conditions. For those analyses where partial observations are mixed with complete observations, results from full subplots (or plots) can be reported as "interior" or "intact" forested conditions and partial observations can be reported as "edge" conditions, although additional information regarding plot proximity to roads or other human disturbance might be used to verify the degree of fragmentation that may influence plant composition. Comparisons among observations of mixed sizes must be qualified with the number of subplots and quadrats sampled, and the presence or absence of any nonforested areas on the plot.

Also, as previously noted, the VEG indicator ignores boundaries between different forested conditions when such boundaries bisect a subplot. However, depending on how a domain of interest is defined, a plot with multiple condition classes may be within a single domain of interest. On the other hand, restricting analyses to a specific domain (e.g., a particular forest type) may reduce a complete observation to a partial observation. Options for handling subplots or plots that are not fully within the domain of interest include:

1. Assigning the subplot (or plot) to the condition at subplot center and assuming that species are distributed evenly across all forested conditions located there.
2. Identifying subplots (or plots) with mixed forest conditions by labeling them as such.
3. Excluding mixed observations from the analysis.

Analysts may consider calculating all approaches and comparing results. When reporting, results should be qualified with the approach used.

For those estimators where it is acceptable to use partial plots or partial subplots, it may occasionally happen that a plot or subplot straddles a population boundary. When this occurs, n is incremented by 1 if any portion of that plot or subplot cluster is in the population of interest. Note that n is incremented by 1 even if no portion of a cluster is in the domain of interest, as long as the cluster is in the population of interest.

When comparing the distribution of several species, frequencies are most informative when all three levels (quadrat, subplot, plot) are reported from the same plot or population.

Species-Based Estimator Details

Frequency—

Frequency is the proportion of sample units where a species was found compared to the number of sample units measured. Frequency can be reported on a quadrat, subplot, or plot basis, but requires a standard sample area at each level. When comparing the distribution of several species, frequencies are most informative when all three levels are reported from the same plot or population. The frequency estimators presented below may also be expressed as estimates of constancy, where the proportions are multiplied by 100 to convert them to percentages.

Plot-level frequency on a quadrat basis—Frequency at the quadrat level provides the finest detail about the distribution of a species across a plot. For example, a physically small species may have minimal canopy cover, but individuals may be spread widely over the plot. The ROM estimator for plot-level quadrat frequency is

$$\hat{f}_{is} = \frac{\sum_{j=1}^{n} y_{ij}}{\sum_{j=1}^{n} x_{ij}} \tag{3}$$

where

$\hat{f}_{is}$ = the proportion of quadrats where species s is observed in the domain of interest on plot i,

$$y_{ij} = \sum_{q=1}^{3} \delta_{ijq} I_{ijqs} = \text{the number of quadrats where species s is present in the domain}$$
of interest on subplot j of plot i,

$$x_{ij} = \sum_{q=1}^{3} \delta_{ijq} = \text{the number of quadrats in the domain of interest on subplot } j \text{ of}$$
plot i,

δ_{ijq} = a zero-one domain indicator function, that is 1 if quadrat q of subplot j of plot i is within the domain of interest, 0 otherwise. Because only accessible forest is sampled, the domain of interest must be accessible forest, or some subset thereof (such as a particular forest type),

I_{ijqs} = a zero-one species indicator function that is 1 if species s is present on quadrat q of subplot j of plot i, 0 otherwise, and

n = the number of subplots on plot i in the population of interest, which is usually four unless the plot straddles a population boundary.

The variance of equation (3) is estimated by replacing the c subscripts in equation (2) with ij subscripts and the index of summation with j (to specify that the clusters being summed are subplots on plot i), and supplying the appropriate values for y_{ij}, x_{ij}, and n.

Population-level frequency on a quadrat basis—At the population level, quadrat frequency is calculated as:

$$\hat{F}_s = \frac{\sum_{i=1}^{n} y_i}{\sum_{i=1}^{n} x_i} \tag{4}$$

where

$\hat{F}_s$ = the proportion of quadrats where species s is observed in the domain of interest in the population of interest,

$$y_i = \sum_{j=1}^{4} \sum_{q=1}^{3} \delta_{ijq} I_{ijqs} = \text{the number of quadrats where species } s \text{ is present in the}$$
domain of interest on plot i,

$$x_i = \sum_{j=1}^{4} \sum_{q=1}^{3} \delta_{ijq} = \text{the number of quadrats in the domain of interest on plot } i,$$
the indicator functions δ_{ijq} and I_{ijqs} remain as defined in equation (3), and
n = the number of plots in the population of interest.

The variance of equation (4) is estimated by replacing the c subscripts in equation (2) with i subscripts (to specify that the clusters being summed are plots), and supplying the appropriate values for y_i, x_i, and n. Unless otherwise noted, the variances of the remaining estimators are calculated similarly—by replacing the c

subscripts in equation (2) with ij or i and index of summation with j or i to specify whether subplots or plots are being summed, respectively.

Plot-level frequency on a full subplot basis—Although quadrat frequency has the potential to provide the most detail about the spatial distribution of a species, if a distribution is clumped, the species may occur less frequently on quadrats than it would if evenly dispersed. Subplot frequency can provide more information for these species. Only subplots that are 100-percent within the domain of interest are included for this estimator because it is important for observational units to be of uniform area. Note that the 100-percent specification is not necessary for quadrats because quadrats are too small to map, and are therefore measured as all in or all out of any given domain or population. Subplot frequency is calculated as

$$\hat{f}'_{is} = \frac{\sum\limits_{j=1}^{n} y_{ij}}{\sum\limits_{j=1}^{n} x_{ij}} \tag{5}$$

where

$\hat{f}'_{is}$ = the proportion of full subplots where species s is observed in the domain of interest on plot i,

$y_{ij} = \delta_{ij} \mathrm{I}_{ijs}$,

$x_{ij} = \delta_{ij}$,

I_{ijs} = a zero-one species indicator function that is 1 if species s is present on subplot j of plot i, 0 otherwise,

δ_{ij} = a zero-one domain indicator function that is 1 if subplot j of plot i is 100 percent within the domain of interest, 0 otherwise. Because only accessible forest is sampled, the domain of interest must be accessible forest, or some subset thereof. If a subset (such as a particular forest type) is specified, the subplot must be 100 percent within the specified subset, and

n = the number of subplots on plot i, which is usually four unless the plot straddles a population boundary.

Population-level frequency on a full subplot basis—At the population level, subplot frequency is calculated as:

$$\hat{F}'_s = \frac{\sum\limits_{i=1}^{n} y_i}{\sum\limits_{i=1}^{n} x_i} \tag{6}$$

where

$\hat{F}'_s$ = the proportion of subplots where species s is observed in the domain of interest in the population of interest,

$y_i = \sum_{j=1}^{4} \delta_{ij} I_{ijs}$ = the number of subplots where species s is present in the domain of interest on plot i,

$x_i = \sum_{j=1}^{4} \delta_{ij}$ = the number of subplots in the domain of interest on plot i,

the indicator functions δ_{ij} and I_{ijs} remain as defined for equation (5), and

n = the number of plots in the population of interest.

Population-level frequency on a full plot basis—This estimator is limited to plots where all four subplots are completely within the domain of interest:

$$\hat{F}_s'' = \frac{\sum_{i=1}^{n} y_i}{\sum_{i=1}^{n} x_i} \qquad (7)$$

where

$\hat{F}_s''$ = the proportion of plots where species s is observed in the domain of interest in the population of interest,

$y_i = \delta_i I_{is}$,

$x_i = \delta_i$,

I_{is} = a zero-one species indicator function that is 1 if species s is present on plot i, 0 otherwise,

δ_i = a zero-one species indicator function that is 1 if plot i is 100 percent within the domain of interest, 0 otherwise. Because only accessible forest is sampled, the domain of interest must be accessible forest or some subset thereof. If a subset (such as a particular forest type) is specified, the plot must be 100 percent within the specified subset, and

n = the number of plots in the population of interest.

Frequency on all-subplots basis or all-plot basis—For some applications, it is useful to relax the 100-percent restriction on the domain of interest for the frequency estimators specified in equations (5), (6), and (7). The equations remain the same, but the domain indicators δ_{ij} or δ_i are 1 on all subplots or plots that are fully or partially in the domain of interest, and 0 otherwise. This allows the use of data from partial subplots, which may reveal information about species that are found more often on the edges of the forest. However, these revised estimators violate the rule of uniform areas, and should therefore be used with caution; for most analyses involving frequency only full sample units are included. Some estimators described later in this section do not require the 100-percent restriction. Primes are added to the domain indicators that do not require the 100-percent restriction (e.g., δ_{ij}').

Canopy cover is recorded at the subplot level as both total cover and cover by layer.

Species abundance—

Species canopy cover for any species, as a measure of species abundance, is recorded directly in the field, within a range of trace (0.1 percent) up to 100 percent, in increments of 1 percent. Canopy cover is recorded at the subplot level as both total cover and cover by layer.

Vegetation information is not collected on nonforest plots or the nonforested portions of partially forested plots. Boundaries between forested conditions (which differ by some factor such as structural stage or community type) are ignored at the subplot level. Any of the options described thus far for handling subplots that are not fully within the domain of interest also apply to the abundance estimators discussed here.

For partial subplots, the percentage of cover recorded in the field relates to the standard subplot area. For example, a species with cover over a 4- by 4-ft square is about 1 percent cover for a full subplot. If the subplot is only 50-percent forested, the field crew would still enter 1 percent for the species. Because no observations are recorded in nonforest or inaccessible conditions, the cover estimates must be adjusted to correctly represent the portion of a subplot in accessible forest. So for the above example where 1 percent cover is recorded for a subplot that is 50 percent forest, the adjustment to 2 percent cover (2 percent of the forested portion) is made in the equations below by placing adj_{ij} in the denominator of y_{ij}.

Average aerial species cover—Aerial cover refers to the two-dimensional cover of a species as seen from above.

Plot-level species cover—Plot-level estimates of average subplot cover by species s, which are especially useful for display in mapped products, are calculated as follows:

$$\hat{c}_{is} = \frac{\sum\limits_{j=1}^{n} y_{ij}}{\sum\limits_{j=1}^{n} x_{ij}} \tag{8}$$

where

$\hat{c}_{is}$ = the mean percentage cover of species s in the domain of interest on plot i,

$y_{ij} = \dfrac{c_{ijs}\delta'_{ij}}{adj_{ij}}$ = the percentage cover of species s in the domain of interest of

subplot j of plot i, adjusted to represent cover on the portion of the subplot in accessible forest,

c_{ijs} = the percentage cover of species s in the accessible forest portion of subplot j of plot i, based on the standard subplot area,

adj_{ij} = the proportion of subplot j of plot i, in accessible forest,

δ'_{ij} = a zero-one domain indicator function that is 1 if subplot j of plot i contains a domain of interest, 0 otherwise. Note that the cover estimate is assumed to be evenly distributed across all forested domains on subplot j of plot i.

$x_{ij} = \delta'_{ij}$, and

n = the number of subplots on plot i in the population of interest, which is usually four unless the plot straddles a population boundary.

Population-level species cover—Average cover of a species at the population level is estimated as the ratio of cover to forest area, as described below. Users are cautioned that variances will be high, especially when the population is broadly defined (e.g., the total area of a species over a state or region). Most species occur in low abundance; there may be many plots where the species was not recorded. Variances may be reduced when the population is subdivided into more specific domains of interest (e.g., the cover of a species in red pine plantations in Michigan within a particular ecological province).

This estimator can also be used to summarize and describe floristic composition in plant community types where the species of interest has been observed. To calculate the average species cover where recorded, the domain of interest is defined as subplots where the species of interest has been recorded within the population under inquiry.

At the population level, cover is calculated as:

$$\hat{C}_s = \frac{\sum\limits_{i=1}^{n} y_i}{\sum\limits_{i=1}^{n} x_i} \tag{9}$$

where

$\hat{C}_s$ = the mean percentage cover of species s in the domain of interest in the population of interest,

$y_i = \sum\limits_{j=1}^{4} \dfrac{c_{ijs}\delta'_{ij}}{adj_{ij}}$ = the sum (across all subplots) of the percentage canopy cover of species s in the domain of interest on plot i, adjusted to represent the cover of each subplot in accessible forest.

$x_i = \sum\limits_{j=1}^{4} \delta'_{ij}$ = the sum of subplots on plot i that contain a domain of interest,

c_{ijs} and δ'_{ij} are as defined in equation (8), and

n = the number of plots in the population of interest.

Average species cover by layer—

Plot-level species cover by layer—The objective of this estimator is to describe how a species is distributed throughout the height layers on the subplots. The calculation of $\hat{c}_{ils}$ (the mean percentage cover of species s in layer l in the domain of interest of plot i), is the same as equation (8) except:

$$y_{ij} = \frac{c_{ijls}\delta'_{ij}}{adj_{ij}} = \text{the percentage cover of species } s \text{ in layer } l \text{ of subplot } j \text{ of plot } i \text{ in}$$

the domain of interest, adjusted to represent cover on the portion of the subplot in accessible forest, where

c_{ijls} = the percentage cover of species s in the accessible forest portion of layer l of subplot j of plot i, based on the standard plot area.

Population-level species cover by layer—At the population level, the calculation of $\hat{C}_{ls}$ (the mean percentage cover of species s in layer l of the domain of interest in the population of interest) is the same as equation (9) except :

$$y_i = \sum_{j=1}^{4} \frac{c_{ijls}\delta'_{ij}}{adj_{ij}} = \text{the sum (across all subplots) of the percentage canopy cover of}$$

species s in layer l in the domain of interest on plot i, adjusted to represent cover on the portion of each subplot in accessible forest.

Community-Based Estimator Details

Diversity and structure estimators describe the area sampled for scales ranging from an individual stand to a larger population. Diversity measures are directly related to species composition, and so are derived from species matrices. Structure is defined as the vertical arrangement of vascular plants as well as information collected to describe the soil/air interface.

Species matrices are summarized to report diversity in terms of species richness and differential diversity (compositional change) across a plot or a population.

Diversity—

Species matrices are summarized to report diversity in terms of species richness and differential diversity (compositional change) across a plot or a population.

Average species richness (alpha) can be estimated at multiple scales: quadrat (α), subplot (α') and plot levels (α''). Species richness is reported for standard areas of uniform size because numbers of species cannot be assumed to be linearly related to area (Whittaker et al. 2001). Therefore, only sampling units that are 100-percent within the domain of interest are included in order to maintain a standard area (3.28 ft^2 [1 m^2], 1/24 acre, or 1/6 acre).

The total number of species recorded for a plot or population, gamma (γ), is reported with the total area sampled. Plot-to-plot comparisons of plot-level gamma should be limited to plots of equal forested area. Comparisons of population-level gammas with unequal sample sizes should employ rarefaction methods to achieve equal sizes, as described below in the "Gamma" section.

Alpha and gamma are also summarized by species' origin and level of identification; e.g., number of introduced species, native species, and plants not identified to species but recognized as unique from other identified species on a plot (table 4).

Differential diversity is reported as beta, but the species matrix, containing both composition and abundance data, provides information for additional pattern and trend analysis beyond standard estimations.

Species richness—

Alpha—The average number of species occupying a fixed-size area (defined by quadrats, full subplots, or full plots) is used to display and compare species richness from plot to plot or population to population.

Plot-level alpha on a quadrat basis—The estimator $\hat{\alpha}_i$ (the mean number of species per quadrat in the domain of interest on plot i) is the same as specified in equation (3) except:

$$y_{ij} = \sum_{q=1}^{3} \delta_{ijq} S_{ijq} = \text{the sum of species totals from all quadrats in the domain of}$$

interest on subplot j of plot i, where

S_{ijq} = the total number of species tallied on quadrat q of subplot j of plot i.

Population-level alpha on a quadrat basis—At the population level, quadrat-level alpha $\hat{A}$ (the mean number of species recorded per quadrat in the domain of interest in the population of interest) is calculated as specified in equation (4) except:

$$y_i = \sum_{j=1}^{4} \sum_{q=1}^{3} \delta_{ijq} S_{ijq} = \text{the sum of species totals from all quadrats in the domain of}$$

interest on plot i.

Plot-level alpha on a full-subplot basis—As with most previously discussed estimators, this plot-level species-richness metric can only be compared using subplots of uniform size (i.e., 100 percent within the domain of interest). At the plot level, $\hat{\alpha}_i'$ (the mean number of species recorded per full subplot in the domain of interest in the population of interest) is calculated as specified in equation (5) except:

$y_{ij} = \delta_{ij} S_{ij}$ = the sum of species totals from all full subplots in the domain of interest on plot i, where

S_{ij} = the total number of species tallied on subplot j of plot i.

Population-level alpha on a full-subplot basis—At the population level, $\hat{A}'$ (the mean number of species recorded per full subplot in the domain of interest in the population of interest) is calculated the same as equation (6) except:

$$y_i = \sum_{j=1}^{4} \delta_{ij} S_{ij} = \text{the sum of species totals from all full subplots in the domain of}$$

interest on plot i.

Plot-level alpha on a full-plot basis—Plot-level alpha on a full-plot basis is not estimated, but observed directly:

$$\alpha_i'' = \delta_i S_i \qquad (10)$$

where
α_i'' = plot alpha, the total number of unique species recorded on plot i,
S_i = the total number of species tallied on plot i, and
δ_i = 1 if plot i is 100 percent within the domain of interest, 0 otherwise. Because only accessible forest is sampled, the domain of interest must be accessible forest, or some subset thereof. If a subset (such as a particular forest type) is specified, the subplot must be 100 percent within the specified subset.

Because α_i'' is measured directly and not estimated, its variance is zero.

Population-level alpha on a full-plot basis—At the population level, the calculation of Â'' (the mean number of species recorded per full plot in the domain of interest in the population of interest) is the same as equation (7) except:
$y_i = \delta_i S_i$
where S_i = the total number of species tallied on plot i.

Gamma—Gamma (γ) is defined as the total number of unique species codes recorded in a population of interest (or a domain of interest within a population of interest). Estimates of gamma can relate to any size area, but comparisons among gammas must involve areas of similar size because species richness and area are not linearly related. The fixed-size areas of most interest here include plots and populations. Plot-level differences can be addressed by restricting the analysis to full plots. At the population level, estimates of gamma must be adjusted for differences in the sizes of the areas sampled.

Rarefaction—When comparing the species richness (alpha or gamma) of two or more regions or domains, sample size differences must be addressed. It is expected that sample sets (representing regions or domains) with more sample units, and therefore a larger total sample area would include more species, so direct comparison of the number of species found in each region is not appropriate. Rarefaction methods should be used to equalize the sample sets (Gotelli and Colwell 2001, Koellner et al. 2004). The rarefaction method enables comparison of the number of species found in two regions when the sampled areas are unequal. Rarefaction uses the data from the larger sample to estimate how many species would have been found in a smaller sample. If *n* plots are inventoried in the less-sampled region, rarefaction takes a number of hypothetical subsets of *n* plots from the more-sampled region and calculates the average number of species from *n* plots. This average can be compared to the number of species actually found in the less-sampled region. See Colwell et al. (2004) for a demonstration of how rarefaction is derived and used to equalize population sizes.

Nonparametric adjustment—Aside from adjusting for areas of different size, gamma is usually adjusted to correct for unobserved species, which are a factor in any inventory. Parametric methods to adjust gamma are lacking, but nonparametric methods can estimate the "true" number of species, shown below as jackknife methods.

Species richness estimates must acknowledge that some species go undetected.

Species richness estimates must acknowledge that some species go undetected. Indeed, our sampling extent and focus cannot begin to approach the true number of species in a population. However, there are many ways to estimate the "true" number of species within a community of interest (Colwell and Coddington 1994) including extrapolating from species-area curves, parametric methods that are dependent on counts of individuals, and nonparametric estimators.

Nonparametric estimators have proven very useful for estimating the true number of species in plant inventories (Chazdon et al. 1998, Colwell and Coddington 1994) because they avoid assumptions about species distribution and discovery rates (Chao 2005). Several methods require only incident data (presence/absence) and are based on the number of rare or infrequent species:

- First-order jackknife methods base this estimate of the "true" number of species on the number of "rare" species; those species that are only recorded on a single plot (reduces bias of a biased estimator) (Chao 2005, Heltshe and Forrester 1983, McCune and Grace 2002, Scheller and Mladenoff 2002).

- Second-order jackknife methods incorporate those species found on only one or two plots. Although this method can perform poorly with small sample sizes that have some "doubletons" and no "singletons," it has been shown to be the least biased for small sample sizes (McCune and Grace 2002).

- Incidence-based coverage estimator (ICE) incorporates infrequent species that have been detected 10 or fewer times over all sample units. Chazdon et al. (1998) found ICE to be the best estimator to meet the criteria of (1) independence of sample size (above a minimum threshold), (2) insensitivity to patchiness of species distribution, and (3) insensitivity to sample order.

Of the above three methods, first-order jackknife is recommended for its simplicity. Jackknife estimations of the true number of unique species are computed by considering the number of unique species across all samples except for one. This is calculated n times for a data set containing n samples. See Helthshe and Forrester (1983) for a complete derivation. Many software packages include a routine for first-order jackknife estimates of the true number of species (e.g., Colwell 2005, McCune and Mefford 1999, Seaby and Henderson 2006). As more data become available and unknown codes are standardized, analysts can test the performance of the second-order jackknife and ICE estimators. These estimators can be supplemented with species-area curves (plots of the number of species vs. the number of sample units) as an indicator of how well the sample represents the population of interest.

Beta diversity—

Plot-level beta—Beta is defined as the ratio of gamma to alpha, which is the ratio of species richness of a larger sampled area to the average species richness of the smaller individual samples that compose the larger sample. At the plot level, this ratio indicates similarity of species composition among subplots, reflecting influences of multiple forest types, for example. A beta value of 1 indicates all subplots have the same species. As beta increases there is less similarity between subplots. Using the plot-level alphas described above, plot-level beta is defined as

$$\hat{\beta}_i'' = \frac{\alpha_i''}{\hat{\alpha}_i'} \qquad (11)$$

where

$\hat{\beta}_i'' =$ the ratio of plot-to-subplot species richness for plot i.

Because beta is dependent on area-sensitive estimations, it can only be compared among plots where the numbers of subplots are the same. In general, this will limit the use of plot-level beta to full plots.

Using the notation from equation (11), and assuming there is no covariance between the numerator and denominator, Cochran (1977: sec. 6.19, eq. 6.95) estimated the variance of a ratio of two estimators as

$$\hat{V}\left(\hat{\beta}_i''\right) = \hat{V}\left(\frac{\alpha_i''}{\hat{\alpha}_i'}\right) = \left[\left(\frac{\alpha_i''}{\hat{\alpha}_i'}\right)^2\right] \times \left[\frac{\hat{V}(\alpha_i'')}{(\alpha_i'')^2} + \frac{\hat{V}(\hat{\alpha}_i')}{(\hat{\alpha}_i')^2}\right] \qquad (12)$$

Because $\hat{V}(a_i'') = 0$, equation (12) simplifies to

$$\hat{V}\left(\hat{\beta}_i''\right) = \hat{V}\left(\frac{\alpha_i''}{\hat{\alpha}_i'}\right) = \left[\left(\frac{\alpha_i''}{\hat{\alpha}_i'}\right)^2\right] \times \left[\frac{\hat{V}(\hat{\alpha}_i')}{(\hat{\alpha}_i')^2}\right] \qquad (13)$$

Population-level beta—Population-level beta estimates the similarity of species composition among plots. The closer to 1, the more similar the species composition; the higher the number, the higher the "turnover" in species (or, the more communities included within the population and domain of interest).

Beta diversity is a property of the sample more so than an inherent property of the community (Greig-Smith 1983), as is gamma. If the analysis includes a comparison of betas of two or more populations, sample-based rarefaction estimates of gamma should be used to ensure equal sample areas are compared.

Using the population-level alpha ($\hat{A}''$) described above, population-level beta is defined as

$$\hat{B} = \frac{\hat{\gamma}}{\hat{A}''} \tag{14}$$

where gamma $(\hat{\gamma})$ and its variance are usually estimated with one of the nonparametric techniques discussed previously.

The variance of plot-level beta can be estimated by substituting the appropriate values into equation (12)

$$\hat{V}\left(\hat{B}\right) = \hat{V}\left(\frac{\hat{\gamma}}{\hat{A}''}\right) = \left[\left(\frac{\hat{\gamma}}{\hat{A}''}\right)^2\right] \times \left[\frac{\hat{V}(\hat{\gamma})}{\hat{\gamma}^2} + \frac{\hat{V}\left(\hat{A}''\right)}{\left(\hat{A}''\right)^2}\right] \tag{15}$$

Structure and condition of soil-atmosphere interface—
Plot structure measurements specific to the VEG indicator include total foliar cover by layers and ground cover assessments, both derived from field-recorded ocular estimates. Calculated means may have large variances, depending on how the populations or domains are defined. Variances can be calculated, but ranges may be a more intuitive description of variability of conditions across populations for many users.

Absolute canopy cover by layer—This estimator reflects overall canopy cover of all vascular plant species, assessed without species differentiation, in each layer. This cannot be derived directly from species canopy cover because the various species' foliage or live twigs may or may not overlap. Cover is recorded in 1-percent increments. Similar to the way cover is recorded for species abundance, field crews record cover estimates on a full subplot basis, and these estimates are adjusted for partially forested subplots when the data are processed.

Plot-level average absolute cover by layer—Plot-level average absolute cover by layer $(\hat{c}_{il})$ is calculated as specified in equation (8) except:

Plot structure measurements specific to the VEG indicator include total foliar cover by layers and ground cover assessments, both derived from field-recorded ocular estimates.

$$y_{ij} = \frac{c_{ijl}\delta'_{ij}}{adj_{ij}} = \text{the percentage cover of all vascular plant species in layer } l \text{ of}$$

subplot j of plot i in the domain of interest, adjusted to represent cover on the portion of the subplot in accessible forest, where

c_{ijl} = the percentage cover of all vascular plant species in the accessible forest portion of layer l of subplot j of plot i, based on the standard plot area.

Again, the variances of the cover estimators presented here and below are calculated by substituting the appropriate variables into equation (2).

Population absolute cover by layer—This estimator measures the mean cover of all vascular plants in the population on a subplot basis and is assessed without species differentiation in each layer. This cannot be derived from species canopy cover, as species may or may not overlap. As with species canopy cover, only accessible forested land is assessed, but measures are based on the standard subplot area. Population-level absolute cover by layer ($\hat{C}_l$) is calculated as specified in equation (9) except:

$$y_i = \sum_{j=1}^{4} \frac{c_{ijl}\delta'_{ij}}{adj_{ij}} = \text{the sum (across all subplots) of the percentage canopy cover}$$

of all vascular plant species in layer l of plot i in the domain of interest, adjusted to represent the cover of each subplot in accessible forest.

The domain is always limited to accessible forest land, but could be further limited by attributes of interest such as forest type or ecoregion.

Ground cover—Ground cover variables describe the soil surface conditions on the subplot. These variables include cryptobiotic crust, lichen, litter/duff, mineral soil, moss, rock, standing water (flood), permanent water (streams, lakes), trash, and wood, as defined in the field guide. As with species and absolute canopy cover, these measures are taken in the field based on the standard subplot area and then adjusted for partially forested subplots when the data are processed.

Plot-level ground cover—Plot-level average ground cover ($\hat{c}_{ig}$) is calculated as specified in equation (8) except:

$$y_{ij} = \frac{c_{ijg}\delta'_{ij}}{adj_{ij}} = \text{the percentage ground cover on subplot } j \text{ of plot } i \text{ in the domain}$$

of interest, adjusted to represent cover on the portion of the subplot in accessible forest, where

c_{ijg} = the percentage ground cover on the accessible forest portion of subplot j of plot i, based on the standard plot area.

Population-level ground cover—Population-level absolute cover by layer ($\hat{C}_g$) is calculated as specified in equation (9) except

$$y_i = \sum_{j=1}^{4} \frac{c_{ijg}\delta'_{ij}}{adj_{ij}}$$ = the sum (across all subplots) of the percentage ground cover on

plot i in the domain of interest, adjusted to represent ground cover on the portion of each subplot in accessible forest.

Change Estimation

The FIA Program's sample design of measuring permanent plots results in a powerful means of detecting change, even at the extensive scale of the P3 grid. Change detection is enhanced with permanent plots that are remeasured over time, much more than if randomly selected plots were used (Elzinga et al. 1998). Change can be assessed with both plot- and population-level estimators by calculating the differences in the estimators obtained at time t and time $t+1$. Some estimators will be more directly interpretable than others. For example, changes in a species quadrat frequency between time t and time $t+1$ will reveal if a species is becoming more or less dispersed over plots. A lack of change in species richness over a domain of interest only reveals that the number of species has remained the same, but does not provide any information regarding changes in species composition.

Plot- and population-level estimators at time t and time $t+1$ are compared with paired t-tests for any plot visited at both times when sample size allows (Elzinga et al. 1998, Sokal and Rohlf 1981) or the equivalent nonparametric Wilcoxon signed rank test (Conover 1980, Sokal and Rohlf 1981). If more than two times are available, then this turns into a typical repeated measures analysis where trend over time could be tested along with individual comparisons that would use an experment-wise alpha with the Bonferroni adjustment.

Changes in species richness can be assessed in a straightforward manner by using paired t-tests. Paired t-tests can be used to assess changes in individual species' frequencies at quadrat and subplot levels when the next larger sample level is considered to be the sample unit (i.e., quadrat frequency within subplots or plots, subplot frequency at plot level).

For estimators based on cover measures, paired t-tests can be applied to both raw measures, or raw measures transformed by appropriate methods for the question at hand (McCune and Grace 2002). Both approaches may be used and results compared. Changes in individual species' cover are likely to be most confounded by differences in climatic variation from year to year, and differences in phenological timing of the plot visits. Changes in absolute average percentage canopy cover by layer may be less sensitive to influences based on plot visit timings and climatic variations than is individual species cover, but should still be treated cautiously.

The FIA Program's sample design of measuring permanent plots results in a powerful means of detecting change, even at the extensive scale of the phase 3 grid.

Frequency is the recommended estimator for assessing change in an individual species' distribution.

Changes in ground cover are not expected to be as sensitive to timing of plot visits, but cover percentages may also be converted to classes to acknowledge the differences in observers.

Frequency is the recommended estimator for assessing change in an individual species' distribution, with changes in species cover used as a supplemental descriptor of change in abundance.

The McNemar test statistic (T) can also be used for assessing differences in proportions (such as frequency) when permanent plots are remeasured. This test is most powerful when the observations are highly correlated, as when the same sample units are measured at time t and time $t+1$. With this test, each level of frequency (quadrat, subplot, plot) can be treated as the sampling unit (Elzinga et al. 1998).

$$T = \frac{(b-c)^2}{(b+c)} \qquad (16)$$

where

b = the number of sample (or subsample) units where a species (or group of species) was found in year 1 but not year 2, and

c = the number of sample (or subsample) units where the species (or group of species) was not found in year 1 but found in year 2.

The test statistic (equation 16) is then compared to the chi-square distribution with 1 degree of freedom. The null hypothesis of no change is rejected if the test statistic exceeds the chi-square table value for 1 degree of freedom.

Notation for Equations

Indices

i = plot index, $i = 1, \ldots,$

j = subplot index, $j = 1, \ldots, 4$

q = quadrat index, $q = 1, \ldots, 3$

s = species index, $s = 1, \ldots,$

n = total number of plots in the population of interest (or the number of subplots on a plot when the population of interest is defined as a plot)

l = layer index, defining vertical layer ranges

g = ground cover variable index

Species-Based Estimators

$\hat{f}_{is}$ = **plot-level** frequency on a **quadrat** basis

$\hat{F}_{s}$ = **population-level** frequency on a **quadrat** basis

$\hat{f}'_{is}$ = **plot-level** frequency on a **subplot** basis

$\hat{F}'_{s}$ = **population-level** frequency on a **subplot** basis

$\hat{F}''_{s}$ = **population-level** frequency on a **plot** basis

$\hat{c}_{is}$ = cover, percentage of subplot area averaged at the **plot** level

$\hat{C}_{s}$ = cover, percentage of subplot area averaged at the **population** level

I_s = zero-one species indicator function that is 1 if species s is present, 0 otherwise

Community-Based Estimators

δ = zero-one domain indicator function that is 1 if the sample unit (quadrat, subplot, or plot) is 100 percent within the domain of interest, 0 if otherwise

δ' = zero-one domain indicator function that is 1 if the sample unit (quadrant, subplot, or plot) contains the domain of interest, 0 if otherwise

p_{ij} = the proportion of a subplot in accessible forest condition or within a more restricted domain of interest

α = alpha, species richness of a standard area.

$\hat{\alpha}_i$ = the **plot** average of number of species per **quadrat**

$\hat{A}$ = the **population** average number of species per **quadrat**

$\hat{\alpha}'_i$ = the **plot** average of number of species per full **subplot**

$\hat{A}'$ = the **population** average number of species per full **subplot**

α''_i = the **total** number of unique species on a full **plot**

$\hat{A}''$ = the **population** average number of species per full **plot**

$\hat{\beta}$ = beta, ratio of gamma to alpha representing similarity (difference) in plant species composition across a **plot**

$\hat{B}$ = beta, ratio of gamma to alpha representing similarity (difference) in plant species composition across a **population**

S = total number of unique species recorded on a full sample unit (quadrat, subplot, or plot)

γ = gamma, the total number of unique species tallied in the population of interest

Acknowledgments

The Vegetation Diversity and Structure indicator began as an interagency effort within the Forest Health Monitoring Program in the mid-1990s. Significant early contributions to the development of this indictor were made by Martin Stapanian, Ken Stolte, Tom Stohlgren, Kelly Rimar, Florence Peterson, and Rick Shory. In more recent years, Andrew Gray, Katherine Johnson, Cassandra Olson, Sarah Butler, Darin Toone, and Cyndi Herbert have been key players in refining methods and assuring quality data are collected. Special attention to data management has been essential, and the author is in debt to Kevin Dobelbower, Lisa Mahal, Jane Reid, and Chuck Veneklase for their clear vision of required detail for quality data stewardship.

The author also thanks the many reviewers who have guided the development and documentation of this indicator, including various FIA personnel and anonymous reviewers. Special thanks to Tara Barrett and Vicente Monleon of the PNW Research Station, Forest Inventory and Analysis Program for their thoughtful review and patient statistical guidance. Thanks also to Dave Allen of Chugach National Forest for designing figures 1, 2, and 3. The author also appreciates the attention to detail given to this document by Lynn Sullivan, technical editor with the PNW research Station's Communications and Applications Group.

Metric Equivalents

When you know:	Multiply by:	To find:
Feet (ft)	0.305	Meters (m)
Square feet (ft^2)	.0929	Square meters (m^2)
Acres	.405	Hectares

Literature Cited

Bailey, R.G. 1995. Description of the ecoregions of the United States. 2nd ed. Misc. Publ. N. 1391, Map scale 1:7,500,000. Washington, DC: U.S. Department of Agriculture, Forest Service. 108 p.

Bechtold, W.A.; Patterson P.L., eds. 2005. The enhanced Forest Inventory and Analysis Program–national sampling design and estimation procedures. Gen. Tech. Rep. SRS-80. Asheville, NC: U.S. Department of Agriculture, Forest Service, Southern Research Station. 85 p.

Boggs, K. 2000. Classification of community types, successional sequences, and landscapes of the Copper River Delta, Alaska. Gen. Tech. Rep. PNW-GTR-469. Portland OR: U.S. Department of Agriculture, Forest Service, Pacific Northwest Research Station. 244 p.

Chao, A. 2005. Species richness estimation. In: Balakrishnan, N.; Read, C.B.; Vidakovic, B., eds. Encyclopedia of statistical sciences. 2nd ed. New York: John Wiley and Sons, Inc.: 7907-7916. Vol. 12.

Chao, A.; Cazdon, R.L.; Colwell, R.K.; Shen, T-J. 2005. A new statistical approach for assessing similarity of species composition with incidence and abundance data. Ecology Letters. 8: 148-159.

Chao, A.; Hwang, W.-H.; Chen, Y.-C.; Kau, C.-Y. 2000. Estimating the number of shared species in two communities. Statistica Sinca. 10: 227-246.

Chazdon, R.L.; Colwell, R.K.; Denslow, J.S.; Guariguata, M.R. 1998. Statistical methods for estimating species richness of woody regeneration in primary and secondary rain forests of northeastern Costa Rica. In: Dallmeier, F.; Comiskey, J.A., eds. Forest biodiversity research, monitoring, and modeling: conceptual background and Old World case studies. Paris: Parthenon Publishing: 285-309.

Cleland, D.T.; Freeouf, J.A.; Keys, J.E.; Nowacki, G.J.; Carpenter, C.A.; McNab, W.H. 2005. Ecological subregions; sections and subsections for the conterminous United States. Map on CD-ROM [1:3,500,000]. (A.M. Sloan, cartographer) Washington, DC: U.S. Department of Agriculture, Forest Service.

Cochran, W.G. 1977. Sampling techniques. 3rd ed. New York: John Wiley and Sons, Inc. 428 p.

Colwell, R.K. 2005. EstimateS: statistical estimation of species richness and shared species from samples. Version 7.5. User's Guide and application. http://purl.oclc. org/estimates. (July 15, 2008).

Colwell, R.K.; Coddington, J.A. 1994. Estimating terrestrial biodiversirty through extrapolation. Philosophical Transactions of the Royal Society of London B. 345: 101-118.

Colwell, R.K.; Xuan Mao, C.; Chang, J. 2004. Interpolating, extrapolating, and comparing incidence-based species accumulation curves. Ecology. 85: 2717-2727.

Conkling, B.L.; Coulston, J.W.; Ambrose, M.J., eds. 2005. Forest health monitoring: 2001 national technical report. Gen Tech. Rep. SRS-81. Asheville, NC: U.S. Department of Agriculture, Forest Service, Southern Research Station. 204 p.

Conover, W.J. 1980. Practical nonparametric statistics. New York: John Wiley and Sons, Inc. 493 p.

Cooperrider, A.Y.; Boyd, R.J.; Stuart, H.R., eds. 1986. Inventory and monitoring of wildlife habitat. Denver, CO: U.S. Department of the Interior, Bureau of Land Management, Service Center. 858 p.

Crawley, M.J.; Harrel, J.E. 2001. Scale dependence in plant biodiversity. Science: 291: 864-868.

Daubenmire, R. 1959. A canopy-coverage method of vegetation analysis. Northwest Science. 33(1): 43-63.

DeVelice, R.L.; Hubbard, C.J.; Boggs, K.; Boudreau, S.; Potkin, M.; Boucher, T.; Wertheim, C. 1999. Plant community types of the Chugach National Forest: southcentral Alaska. Tech. Publ. R10-TP-76. Anchorage, AK: U.S. Department of Agriculture, Forest Service. Chugach National Forest. 375 p.

Elzinga, C.L.; Salzer, D.W.; Willoughby, J. 1998. Measuring and monitoring plant populations. Technical Reference 1730-1. Denver, CO: U.S. Department of the Interior, Bureau of Land Management. 477 p.

Faber-Langendoen, D.; Menard, S. 2006. A key to eastern forests of the United States: macrogroups, groups, and alliances. Arlington, VA: NatureServe. 78 p.

Federal Geographic Data Committee [FGDC]. 2007. National vegetation classification standard, version 2–working draft. FDGC-STD-005. Reston, VA: Vegetation Subcommittee, FGDC Secretariat, U.S. Geological Survey. 124 p. http://www.fgdc.gov/4/projects/FGDC-standards-projects/vegetation/ (November 23, 2007).

Frelich, L.E.; Machado, J.; Reich, P.B. 2003. Fine-scale environmental variation and structure of understory plant communities in two old-growth pine forests. Journal of Ecology. 91: 283-293.

Gotelli, N.J.; Colwell, R.K. 2001. Quantifying biodiversity: procedures and pitfalls in the measurement and comparison of species richness. Ecology Letters. 4: 379-391.

Gray, A.N.; Azuma, D.L. 2005. Repeatability and implementation of a forest vegetation indicator. Ecological Indicators. 5(2005): 57-71.

Greenough, J.A. 2001. Fuel characteristic classification system design. Prepared by ESSA Technologies Ltd., Vancouver, BC, for USDA Forest Service. 48 p. On file with: D. Sandberg, Forestry Sciences Lab, 3200 SW Jefferson Way, Corvallis, OR 97331.

Greig-Smith, P. 1983. Quantitative plant ecology. 3rd ed. Berkly, CA: University of California Press. 347 p.

Hatton, T.J.; West, N.E.; Johnson, P.S. 1986. Relationship of the error associated with ocular estimation and actual total cover. Journal of Range Management. 39: 91-92.

Heinz Center. 2006. Filling the gaps: priority data needs and key management challenges for national reporting on ecosystem condition. Washington, DC: H. John Heinz Center for Science, Economics and the Environment. 104 p.

Helm, D.; Mead, B. 2004. Reproducibility of vegetation cover estimates in south-central Alaska forests. Journal of Vegetation Science. 14: 33-40.

Heltshe, J.F.; Forrester, N.E. 1983. Estimating species richness using the jackknife procedure. Biometrics. 39: 1-11.

Ingerson, A.; Loya, W. 2008. Measuring forest carbon: strengths and weaknesses of available tools summary. Science and Policy Brief. Washington, DC: The Wilderness Society. 20 p. http://wilderness.org/Library/briefs.cfm. (July 24, 2008).

Jaccard, P. 1901. Etude comparative de la distribution florale dans une portion des Alpes et des Jura. [A study comparing the distribution of flora in a portion of the Jura Alps] Bulletin. Societe Vaudoise des Sciences Natirelles. 37: 547-579.

Jennings, M.D.; Faber-Langendoen, D.; Peet, R.K.; Loucks, O.L.; Glenn-Lewin, D.C.; Damman, A.; Barbour, M.G.; Pfister, R.; Grossman, D.H.; Roberts, D.; Tart, D.; Walker, M.; Talbot, S.S.; Walker, J.; Hartshorn, G.S; Waggoner, G.; Abrams, M.D.; Hill, A.; Rejmanek, M. 2006. Description, documentation, and evaluation of associations and alliances within the U.S. National Vegetation Classification, Version 4.5. Washington, DC: Ecological Society of America, Vegetation Classification Panel. 119 p.

Johnson, C.G., Jr.; Swanson, D.K. 2005. Bunchgrass plant communities of the Blue and Ochoco Mountains: a guide for managers. Gen. Tech. Rep. PNW-GTR-641. Portland OR: U.S. Department of Agriculture, Forest Service, Pacific Northwest Research Station. 119 p.

Jukola-Sulonen, E.; Salemaa, M. 1985. A comparison of different sampling methods of quantitative vegetation analysis. Silva Fennica. 19(3): 325-337.

Kenkel, K.A.; Podani, J. 1991. Plot size and estimation efficiency in plant community studies. Journal of Vegetation Science. 2: 539-544.

Kennedy, K.A.; Addison, P.A. 1987. Some considerations for the use of visual estimates of plant cover in biomonitoring. Journal of Ecology. 75: 151-157.

Klinka, K.; Krajina, V.J.; Ceska, A.; Scagel, A.M. 1989. Indicator plants of coastal British Columbia. Vancouver, BC: UBC Press, University of British Columbia. 288 p.

Koellner, T.; Herserger, A.M.; Wohlgemuth, T. 2004. Rarefaction method for assessing plant species diversity on a regional scale. Ecography. 27: 532-544.

Ludwig, J.A.; Reynolds, J.F. 1988. Statistical ecology. New York: John Wiley and Sons, Inc. 337 p.

Lutes, D.; Keane, R.; Key, C.; Caratti, J.; Gangi, L.; Couch, C. 2003. FIREMON: Fire Effects Monitoring and Inventory Protocol. http://fire.org/index.php?option=content&task=section&id=5&Itemid=42. (January 3, 2008).

MacArthur, R.H.; MacArthur, J.W. 1961. On bird species diversity. Ecology. 42(3): 594-598.

McCune, B.; Grace, J.B. 2002. Analysis of ecological communities. Gleneden Beach, OR: MjM Software Design. 300 p.

McCune, B.; Mefford, M.J. 1999. PC-ORD. Multivariate analysis of ecological data. Version 5. Gleneden Beach, OR: MjM Software Design. 237 p.

Mueller-Dombois, D.; Ellenberg, H. 1974. Aims and methods of vegetation ecology. New York: John Wiley and Sons, Inc. 547 p.

Nygaard, P.H.; Ødegaard, T. 1999. Sixty years of vegetation dynamics in a south boreal coniferous forest in southern Norway. Journal of Vegetation Science. 10: 5-16.

Pausas, J.G.; Austin, M.P. 2001. Patterns of plant species richness in relation to different environments: an appraisal. Journal of Vegetation Science. 12: 153-166.

Pitkanen, S. 1997. Correlation between stand structure and ground vegetation: an analytical approach. Plant Ecology. 131: 109-126.

Pitkanen, S. 1998. The use of diversity indices to assess the diversity of vegetation in managed boreal forests. Forest Ecology and Management. 112: 121-137.

Riitters, K.; Tkacz, B. 2004. Forest health monitoring. In: Wiersma, B., ed. Environmental monitoring. Boca Raton, FL: CRC Press: 669-683

Rudis, V.A. 1991. Wildlife habitat, range, recreation, hydrology and related research using Forest Inventory and Analysis surveys: a 12-year compendium.

Gen. Tech. Rep. SO-84. New Orleans, LA: U.S. Department of Agriculture, Forest Service, Southern Forest Experiment Station. 61 p.

Rudis, V.A. 2003. Comprehensive regional resource assessments and multipurpose uses of Forest Inventory and Analysis data, 1976 to 2001: a review. Gen. Tech. Rep. SRS-70. Asheville, NC: U.S. Department of Agriculture, Forest Service, Southern Research Station. 129 p.

SAS Institute Inc. 2004. SAS/STATR 9.1 User's guide. Cary, NC: SAS Institute Inc. 5121 p.

Scheiner, S.M. 1992. Measuring pattern diversity. Ecology. 73: 1860-1867.

Scheiner, S.M. 2003. Six types of species-area curves. Global Ecology and Biogeography. 12: 441-447.

Scheller, R.M.; Mladenoff, D.J. 2002. Understory species patterns and diversity in old-growth and managed northern hardwood forests. Ecological Applications. 12(5): 1329-1343.

Scott, W.A.; Hallam, C.J. 2002. Assessing species misidentification rates through quality assurance of vegetation monitoring. Plant Ecology. 165(1): 101-115.

Seaby, R.M.; Henderson, P.A. 2006. Species diversity and richness. Version 4. Lymington, England: Pisces Conservation Ltd. http://www.pisces-conservation. com/indexsoftdiversity.html. (September 10, 2008).

Smith, S.D.; Bunting, S.C.; Hironaka, M. 1986. Sensitivity of frequency plots for detecting vegetation change. Northwest Science. 60: 279-286.

Smith, W.D.; Conkling, B.I. 2004. Analyzing forest health data. Gen. Tech. Rep. SRS-77. Asheville, NC: U.S. Department of Agriculture, Forest Service, Southern Research Station. 33 p.

Sokal, R.R.; Rohlf, F.J. 1981. Biometry. 2nd ed. San Francisco: W.H. Freeman and Company. 859 p.

Sørenson, T.A. 1948. A method of establishing groups of equal amplitude in plant sociology based on similarity of species content, and its application to analyses of the vegetation on Danish commons. Biologoske Skrifter Kongelige Danske Videnskabernes Selskab. 5: 1-34.

Stapanian, M.A.; Cline, S.P.; Cassell, D.L. 1997. Evaluation of a measurement method for forest vegetation in a large-scale ecological survey. Environmental Monitoring and Assessment. 45: 237-257.

Stohlgren, T.J. 1994. Planning long-term vegetation studies at landscape scales. In: Powell, T.M.; Steele, J.H., eds. Ecological time series. New York: Chapman & Hall: 209-241.

Stolte, K.; Conkling, B.; Campbell, S.; Gillespie, A. 2002. Forest health indicators Bulletin FS-746. Arlington, VA: U.S. Department of Agriculture, Forest Service. 24 p.

Sykes, J.M.; Horril, A.D.; Mountford, M.D. 1983. Use of visual cover estimates as quantitative estimators of some British woodland taxa. Journal of Ecology. 71: 437-450.

Tart, D.; Williams, C.; DiBendedetto, J.; Crow E.; Girard, M.; Gordon, H.; Sleavin, K.; Manning, M.; Haglund, J.; Short, B.; Wheeler, D. 2005. Section 2: Existing vegetation classification protocol. In: Brohman, R.; Bryant, L., eds. Existing vegetation classification and mapping guide. Gen. Tech. Rep. WO-67. Washington, DC: U.S. Department of Agriculture, Forest Service, Ecosystem Management Coordination Staff: 2-1–2-34.

U.S. Department of Agriculture, Forest Service [USDA FS]. 1995. A report to facilitate discussion of indicators of sustainable forest management: a work in progress. Washington, DC. 226 p. http://www.fs.fed.us/land/sustain_dev/sd/sfmsd.htm. (July 23, 2003).

U.S. Department of Agriculture, Forest Service [USDA FS]. 2005. Forest Inventory and Analysis national core field guide. Volume 1: Field data collection procedures for phase 3 plots. Version 3.0. Vol. 2. Washington, DC: Internal report. On file with: U.S. Department of Agriculture, Forest Service, Forestry Sciences Lab, 3041 Cornwallis Rd, Research Triangle Park, NC 27709. http://fia.fs.fed.us/library/field-guides-methods-proc/. (January 3, 2008).

U.S. Department of Agriculture, Natural Resources Conservation Service [USDA NRCS]. 2000. The PLANTS Database. National Plant Data Center, Baton Rouge, LA 70874-4490. http://plants.usda.gov. (January 3, 2008).

van Hees, W.; Mead, B. 2000. Ocular estimates of understory vegetation structure in a closed *i*/ *if* forest. Journal of Vegetation Science. 11: 195-200.

Whittaker, R.H. 1975. Communities and ecosystems. New York: Macmillan Publishing Co., Inc. 385 p.

Whittaker, R.J.; Willis, K.J.; Field, R. 2001. Scale and species richness: towards a general, hierarchical theory of species diversity. Journal of Biogeography. 28: 453-470.

Willis, K.J.; Whittaker, R.J. 2002. Species diversity—scale matters. Science. 295: 1245-1248.

Wilson, M.V.; Shmida, A. 1984. Measuring beta diversity with presence-absence data. Journal of Ecology. 72: 1055-1064.

Zar, J.H. 1996. Biostatistical analysis. 4th ed. Upper Saddle River, NJ: Prentice Hall Inc. 931 p